Roadside
RELICS

AMERICA'S ABANDONED AUTOMOBILES

WILL SHIERS

MOTORBOOKS

Dedication
To the memory of my late grandfather, to whom I owe my love of vehicles.

First published in 2006 by Motorbooks, an imprint of MBI Publishing Company, Galtier Plaza, Suite 200, 380 Jackson Street, St. Paul, MN 55101-3885 USA

MBI Publishing Company titles are also available at discounts in bulk quantity for industrial or sales-promotional use. For details write to Special Sales Manager at MBI Publishing Company, Galtier Plaza, Suite 200, 380 Jackson Street, St. Paul, MN 55101-3885 USA

Editor: Leah Noel
Designer: Maria Friedrich
Cover Designer: Sara Grindle

Printed in China

Library of Congress Cataloging-in-Publication Data

Shiers, Will.
  Roadside relics : America's abandoned automobiles / Will Shiers.
    p. cm.
  ISBN-13: 978-0-7603-2748-7 (hardback with cover)
  ISBN-10: 0-7603-2748-3 (hardback with cover)
  1. Automobiles--United States--Pictorial works. 2. Automobile graveyards--Pictorial works. 3. Shiers, Will. I. Title.
  TL23.S47 2006
  779'.96292220973--dc22
                                        2006013990

Front Cover: In a small rural community somewhere in the Texas Panhandle, an orphaned 1961 Plymouth waits patiently for its owners to return, but it's doubtful that they ever will. Maybe they've passed away, or perhaps they've just walked out on their dilapidated home and car in search of better prospects in the city. Either way, the future looks bleak for both car and house.

Plymouths of this model year looked totally different from the previous year's model; in fact, they looked totally different from anything else on the road. Unfortunately, the controversial styling was not what the public craved, and sales decreased by 44,000 units between 1960 and 1961.

Frontis: Over the years, Mother Nature has carved the beautiful Navajo Twin Rocks in Bluff, Utah, but she has been less kind to this Buick. Although there is little rain in the Four Corners region, owners of old cars in this area need to be wary of the wind. In the desert, it acts like a sandblaster, gradually stripping vehicles to their bare metal.

The perfectly positioned Buick is a 1949 Super four-door sedan, the marque's first redesign after World War II. It was the first time that the instantly identifiable ventiports graced a Buick's fenders.

Although this picture was taken several years ago, I'm reliably informed that this car is still in the same spot today, only in slightly worse condition.

Title Pages: Having finally been persuaded that I wasn't a German spy on a mission to kill him, one of the older residents of Texline, Texas, reluctantly put down the penknife he had been waving in my face and agreed to let me photograph some of the old vehicles on blocks in his yard. He soon realized that I was genuinely interested in photographing old cars and suggested that I go with him into the heart of the Rita Blanca National Grassland, where he knew of some other unwanted wrecks.

Apparently the owners of this 1934 or 1935 Chevrolet Standard Coach left it here many moons ago when they walked out on their homestead and headed west to make their fortune in California. The car has been on its own ever since, apart from the occasional passing hunters, who have emptied a few rounds into it.

Back Cover: When this Cadillac rolled off the production line, it was a thing of beauty and, at $4,569, it was a highly desirable automobile. Who would have guessed that fate would be so unkind and one day it would end up abandoned to the elements in a northern Washington field, burnt out, abused, and riddled with bullet holes?

It's a 1956 Coupe DeVille, one of just over 25,000 to attract a buyer that year. Cadillac was easily America's luxury car sales leader at the time, producing well over 130,000 cars, compared with a combined total of 65,000 for Imperial and Lincoln.

CONTENTS

PREFACE

It's hard to explain my fascination with abandoned cars.

I just think that there's something so poignant about seeing a once-beautiful automobile, a car that used to be someone's pride and joy, sitting lonely in a field or junkyard, abandoned to the elements and ravages of time. The interior once had that unique "new car smell," but now it's cracked and rotting, soiled and torn. The paint and chrome used to be smooth and gleaming, but now they're rusted, pitted, and badly disfigured.

Every vehicle in this book used to be an important part of someone's life—something that was lovingly washed and waxed every Sunday morning. Back then, even the most minor scratch could cause a month-long depression. Yet today, nobody cares.

The photos seen on these pages have been taken during my numerous road trips across the United States during the past ten years. Some of the vehicles shown were found in salvage yards, others in fields, deserts, forests, or ghost towns. I could write another book describing the communities I visited and the people I met while seeking these relics—some who have deliberately isolated themselves and have wonderful tales to tell.

Since these pictures were taken, many of the vehicles have no doubt ended up in that giant junkyard in the sky, crushed and recycled into refrigerators, dishwashers, or perhaps other cars. Of course, a lucky few may have been saved, and others might still be sitting there today, waiting patiently for someone like you to come to their rescue and give them the restoration they so badly deserve.

Hopefully these images will stir some emotions and perhaps trigger some distant memories for you. Maybe you'll remember that sense of freedom you felt when you got behind the wheel of your very first car, or perhaps reminisce over that first kiss at the drive-in movie theater.

Either way, I hope you'll enjoy reading *Roadside Relics: America's Abandoned Automobiles*, as much as I did when taking the pictures.

ACKNOWLEDGMENTS

I would like to thank my father for the hours he has spent tirelessly following me around salvage yards with his notebook and pen in hand, and my mother for letting him come with me. Thanks also to my friends and brother for not complaining too bitterly when I made detours from our planned road trips to salvage yards, ghost towns, and anywhere else I thought abandoned cars might be lurking.

I am indebted to RK Photographic for helping me out with the cost of the film and processing, and to Toby Clark, Tom Chaney, Steve Donaldson, Craig Sheer, and Floyd Nolan for their assistance in identifying some of the less obvious wrecks.

Finally, a special thank you to the owners of all the cars featured here, including the ones whom I was unable to track down.

INTRODUCTION

The search for abandoned, abused, and generally unloved aging vehicles is becoming a challenge. I have been scouring the hedgerows, ghost towns, fields, and junkyards of rural America for old metal for the past decade, but in recent years the pastime has become increasingly difficult.

The rapid disappearance of so much classic tin has a lot to do with China, India, and other emerging markets and their insatiable appetite for steel. Increased demand has pushed scrap-metal prices to an all-time high, and the owners of these cars see dollar signs flashing before their eyes. At the time of this book's writing, scrap was fetching $95 per ton, compared with $7.50 a decade ago. To put this into perspective, a truck loaded with eighteen crushed American cars from the 1960s or 1970s is worth $2,500 today, whereas it would have fetched just $175 in 1996.

For some junkyards' bosses, who also have the added hassle of increased environmental pressures, this is all the impetus they need to get out of the business. Mobile crushers are being called in, cars are being flattened, and money is at last being made. Other junkyard owners are choosing to dispose of part of their stock, and inevitably it's the older, heavier vehicles that are the first to go. While this may sound like killing the goose that lays the golden egg, many will argue that this isn't the case. Elderly cars tend to sit around for years, earning very little income for their owners. The later models, with their quick turnaround of parts, are the serious income generators.

The demand for steel is not going to go away, and the price of recycled metal is likely to remain strong for at least the time being. As the financial pressures intensify on junkyard owners, more and more old cars will be sent to meet their maker. With their demise, we risk losing the traditional junkyards and the valuable service they provide for old-car enthusiasts.

The cars featured in these photographs could soon become only memories of the past.

Salvage yard owners are being forced to comply with an ever-increasing number of regulations regarding the storage and recycling of old vehicles, but back in the 1970s, when these cars were lodged in the bank of Utah's Sevier River, environmental concerns were of little concern to anyone.

CHAPTER 1

FORD

"We don't want tradition. . . . The only history that is worth a tinker's damn is the history we make today."

— Henry J. Ford

I was surprised this 1937 Ford hadn't been snapped up by a hot rodder, but then again it was hidden away in Watts Repair Salvage & Auto of Wymore, Nebraska, which isn't the easiest of yards to find.

The 1937 models were a bit of a milestone for Ford, as they were the company's first cars to adopt an all-steel construction, Ford having finally done away with the old fabric roof inserts. They were also Ford's first cars to have their headlights mounted in the front fenders. This appears to be a Deluxe model, identified by the chrome window surrounds.

This is the scene that greeted me on the approach to Hopkins Antique Autos & Parts of Caldwell, Idaho—a good indication that I wouldn't be finding any of the Nissans, Mazdas, or Toyotas that seem to fill the majority of today's salvage yards. What I did find, however, were several hundred relics dating back to the 1920s, including this Model A Tudor sedan.

This certainly wasn't the only old Ford on the premises, as I discovered a whole row of similarly aged Model As and even a handful of Model Ts dotted around the place.

As well as an incredible collection of cars, Hopkins had numerous barns full of hard-to-find parts, including piles of dashboards, mountains of hubcaps, and row upon row of hoods and doors. In the background, you can make out an area dedicated purely to window surrounds.

I've met some great characters while roaming the countryside hunting for old metal, and one of the best came from the town of Texline, on the Texas/New Mexico border. My elderly friend, who wishes to remain anonymous because he claims to have invented an engine that runs on water and is now in hiding from the oil companies, jumped into my car. This proved to be an unpleasant experience, as he had just been sprayed by a skunk. With the windows unwound, he directed to me to this 1929 Model A coupe.

The car was in the middle of a cornfield, a good few miles from the nearest road, where it has apparently sat for the last fifty years. Just how or why it ended up here is a mystery, although nearby I did discover the remains of a well and the foundation of a forgotten homestead that was abandoned during the Dust Bowl.

This Model A Deluxe coupe, which probably dates back to 1930 or 1931, was found in the Texas Panhandle, on an old stretch of Route 66. Well, I might be glamorizing the truth a little. It was discovered just yards from Interstate 40, on a service road that I presume to be part of the old historic highway. The remaining segments of the world's most famous road are rough and the going is slow, but occasional sights like this make the hard traveling worthwhile.

Despite the harsh winters in this part of the world, what's left of the car is still surprisingly rust free. The gas station in the background has closed down, and I was unable to find anyone to talk to about it.

Fifteen hundred dollars is the asking price for this 1938 Ford Deluxe, which awaits a new owner at the entrance to Windy Hill Auto Parts of New London, Minnesota. That particular production year saw the introduction of two-tier styling, with Deluxe models having a different front from their Standard siblings. The Deluxe featured an attractive curvaceous grille with horizontal bars and separate louvers. Ford sold 101,020 Tudor sedans, all coming with a 60-horsepower V-8 engine.

Although structurally sound, this one is missing quite a bit of glass, which isn't doing the interior any favors. While those twin windshield wipers were an option back in 1938, the turn signals certainly weren't.

When its owner parked this 1938 Ford in a Tennessee forest two years ago, the car was in pristine condition. Okay, that's a total lie, but it is true that foliage significantly accelerates the decaying process of a car.

Trees shade vehicles from the sun, causing a rust-inducing damp environment. A carpet of damp leaves also can drop onto the bodywork in the fall, and in the spring paint-rotting sap drips onto the finish. I have just described the perfect environment for the dreaded tin worm to flourish, and you could almost hear a whole family of them munching their way through this classic.

A few minor trim items are all that's left to salvage.

Above: Anyone wanting to rescue this 1946 Ford is going to need to bring a chain saw because the tree isn't going to give up its companion without a serious fight. And before you shout "Timber!" I suggest that you take a quick look upward because there could well be a 239-cubic-inch V-8 perched precariously on one of the branches above your head. This car was found in an overgrown, seemingly forgotten section of Minnesota's French Lake Auto Parts, otherwise known as Junktown USA.

For its first post–World War II peacetime cars, like most other makes, Ford simply restyled its prewar models. This meant an all-new grille featuring horizontal instead of vertical bars. The styling changes clearly appealed to the car-buying public and allowed Ford to overtake Chevrolet as America's best-selling make—a position it hadn't held since 1937. It was a short-lived victory, though, as Chevrolet was back to top dog the following year.

Left: While traveling south to Carey, Idaho, on Highway 93, just past the Craters of the Moon National Monument, you see a sign that reads "Extreme Flood Hazard." No kidding—just look at what happened to this car. These remains appear to be of a 1941 Ford Tudor sedan, but I am prepared to stand corrected.

I've found dumped cars in some tranquil settings over the years, but this really is one of my favorites. As I approached the banks of the lake, I disturbed a family of ducks that had adopted the car as their home.

Below: You are looking at the distorted remains of what appears to be either a 1946 or 1947 Ford, which has been dragged out of a south Texas woodland to make way for a new housing development. The bulldozer driver clearly had little respect for old cars and was less than considerate in moving this and the 1951 Dodge in the background. Their cruel mistreatment indicates that both are destined for the crusher with no chance for anyone to remove the few salvageable bits of trim.

Above: From the rear, without taillight lenses, 1949, 1950, and 1951 "shoebox" Fords all look identical, so it's difficult to pinpoint the exact vintage of the cars in this lineup.

French Lake Auto Parts of Annandale, Minnesota, where these cars are located, is arguably America's best salvage yard. There are more than 13,000 vehicles at this one hundred–acre site, and they date back to the turn of the last century. Unfortunately, I rolled into the yard just thirty minutes before it was due to close for the night, so I managed to see only a fraction of the amazing vehicles in stock.

Yard owner Floyd Nolan explained that the number of vintage cars on site is actually growing as he buys up the stock of surrounding yards that are either selling out or wanting to concentrate on newer, often more profitable cars. When I visited, he had just taken delivery of a hundred or so vehicles from one such yard, but most were simply too rotten to be of use.

Left: Believe it or not, this 1950 Ford woody will probably live to drive again—at least most of its rear half will. According to Steve Donaldson, the owner of Donaldson's Auto Dismantling in Orange Cove, California, he plans to use this, the remains of another 1950 Country Squire, and a 1949 sedan to create one complete car.

Donaldson's, which has been open for twenty-five years, is incredibly well kept and the only salvage yard I've ever visited with an orange tree on the grounds. And if over the years any antifreeze, oil, gasoline, or transmission fluid has accidentally leaked into the ground, you certainly wouldn't know it by the taste of the fruit.

I would struggle to find this 1950 Ford again, which I was lucky to stumble upon deep in the Tennessee countryside. Although I didn't get too close, for fear of disturbing whatever animal I could hear scurrying around in the undergrowth near the car, it appears to be 99 percent complete. What's more, the rust you would normally expect to find on a car that has sat such a long period of time has yet to take a hold.

It appears to be a Ford Custom Deluxe two-door sedan, which cost a little over $1,500 when it was originally sold in 1950. For this amount, its owner would have been treated to a pair of sun visors, armrests on both doors, and plenty of chrome.

Looking for some hard-to-find parts for your vintage Ford? Then look no further than Antique Auto Ranch of Spokane, Washington. The yard holds about two hundred cars dating from the turn of the twentieth century up to the early 1960s, so you can just imagine what amazing treasures are lurking in this parts barn.

Standing guard outside is a 1952 Ford Country Sedan, the four-door station wagon derivative of the intermediate-trim Customline. At $2,060, this was the most expensive model in the Customline range, and with just under 12,000 finding buyers, it was the least common too.

Claude Holt, the owner of Holt's Auto Salvage, took me for a ride on the back of his ATV—to a far-flung corner of his massive Tennessee salvage yard—to photograph this 1953 Ford. As you can see, the site is severely overgrown, and I made the mistake of wearing shorts and a T-shirt. By the time I was finished, my legs had been ripped to pieces by brambles, attacked by poison ivy, and almost gnawed to the bone by some of the world's most ferocious mosquitoes. (I swear the insects in this yard are far more fierce than any junkyard dog.) Yet it was worth all the pain to get pictures of this car in such a fantastic setting.

The 1953 Ford shared the same body as the 1952 model, only it wore a new grille. This appears to be the Customline, as identified by the chrome window surrounds and the remnants of a chrome strip on the door. Ford celebrated its fiftieth birthday in 1953.

A pitiful excuse for a 1956 Ford Fairlane gradually sinks into the sand in New Mexico, somewhere between Gallup and Naschitti on a Navajo Indian reservation. Whether the car has been buried by someone or the desert has simply engulfed it over the years is unclear. One thing that is certain, though: this vehicle's cruising days are truly over, as it is definitely beyond the hopes and dreams of even the most talented of restorers.

Some 645,000 Fairlanes were bought in 1956, representing close to half of all Fords registered that year.

Below: This 1957 Fairlane was discovered languishing in a yard just a few miles outside of the Lone Star State's capital of Austin. It was one of numerous similarly aged cars, the majority of which looked like they were project rather than parts vehicles.

Of course, the big news from the Ford camp in 1957 was the arrival of the Skyliner, which was christened the only true hardtop convertible in the world. There was also a big battle going on between Ford and Chevy for the number-one sales spot that year; Ford emerged victorious with a record 1.6 million cars built.

Above: The message is clear—"SAVE DON'T CRUSH"—but how much longer can this 1956 Ford Town sedan keep the crusher at bay? It may have just escaped the latest cull in this South Dakota yard, but the price of scrap metal is at an all-time high at the moment, and pretty soon this car is going to be worth more squashed than it is as a parts donor.

Wayne's Auto Salvage in Winner still has a good selection of vintage tin, but today the cars are sparsely spread out over the twenty-acre site.

The four-door Town sedan was by far the biggest seller in the 1956 Fairlane lineup, attracting nearly 245,000 buyers.

Above: Texas has Cadillac Ranch, Nebraska has Carhenge, and Arizona has this unusual auto sculpture in a salvage yard near Phoenix. While I admit that it's not quite as amazing as the great pyramids of Egypt, or even the Luxor in Las Vegas, but as far as pyramids built from cars are concerned, it's up there with the best of them.

Cars like this 1959 Ford station wagon, which is beginning to buckle under the weight, rarely turn up in yards these days. Consequently, those yards that don't specialize in breaking older vehicles are often at a loss as to what to do with them. Their usual clientele is unlikely to need any parts for something this old, so the cars just sit around for years, taking up valuable space. This one is just days from being crushed, having yielded very few parts.

Right: It's difficult to determine how this 1958 Ford Custom 300 ended up in such a sorry state at Wiseman's Auto Salvage of Casa Grande, Arizona, because it doesn't seem to have been involved in any accident. If it had been in a normal head-on collision, then surely the headlights would have been smashed.

At $2,065, the Custom 300 two-door sedan was almost the cheapest car offered by Ford in 1958, undercut only by the Business coupe. Luxury items were few on the vehicle. Buyers were treated to little more than one door armrest and a single sun visor.

Below: Fords manufactured in 1959 are widely considered to be among the most beautiful the company has ever built, although that's hardly a compliment you could bestow on this disheveled wreck. It's a Fairlane four-door sedan, and it was abandoned outside the gate of a Las Vegas salvage yard. I assume its days are numbered, but hopefully somebody will have the good sense to remove the front bumper and some of those sun-baked, rust-free panels before its fate is sealed.

Las Vegas used to have some fantastic yards, but many, like this one, have recently closed down. The proprietor of one of the few surviving businesses that still deals in vintage cars explained that there's no longer any money in the old stuff, and yards are either closing down or concentrating on "rice-burners from Tokyo."

Launched in 1960, the Falcon was Ford's contribution to the compact car market and the company's attempt to ward off the ever-growing number of foreign imports. The car was basically a modern Model A, which was apparently just what the car-buying American public wanted. In its first year of production, 400,000 buyers were attracted to its smaller dimensions, conservative styling, and relatively simple mechanics. The Falcon used a 144-cubic-inch six-cylinder engine that, although simple to maintain, produced a rather uninspiring 90 horsepower. In other words, it took a full eighteen seconds to reach the magical sixty miles per hour.

This example was found abandoned on waste ground somewhere in Alabama.

The 1960 Fairlane was six inches longer, nearly five inches wider, and almost two hundred pounds heavier than its predecessor, but Ford was able to hide the extra bulk with the car's sleek, graceful, yet rather simple styling. Although this was an entry-level car, it still got a splash of chrome here and there, armrests on all four doors, and twin sun visors. This one seems to have an optional roof-mounted external sun visor, too.

It has long since parted company with its engine. Was it the 145-horsepower inline six or the more desirable 185-horsepower V-8 that once sat under its hood? Ford doesn't give an indication of how many of each engine were sold, but more than 110,000 of these four-door sedans rolled off the production line.

The car was discovered at a salvage yard in Fairbury, Nebraska, in spring 2005.

Not everything in black and white makes sense—like why, out of thousands of cars culled from this Minnesota salvage yard, was this pair of 1960 Ford station wagons allowed to survive? Admittedly the Country Squire on the right is something of a rarity, with only 22,237 in production, but that rear-end damage hasn't done it any favors. The black car appears to be a four-door Ranch Wagon, making it more common.

In total, Ford churned out 171,824 wagons in 1960, although there was no breakdown between sixes and V-8s reported.

Vintage Auto Salvage, just off Highway 367, in Bradford, Arkansas, is home to this 1961 Thunderbird and a couple hundred other similarly aged cars and light commercials.

This yard is one of the most unusual that I've come across in that it's more like someone's garden than a junkyard. The six-acre site, which I visited in 2002, is totally unfenced and spread out over the side of a hill. It has a scattering of fruit trees and the kind of well-kept grass that most golf clubs would be proud of, not to mention one of the nicest proprietors in the business, who was happy to let me spend most of a morning roaming the site.

Below: This 1962 Ford Country Sedan may have lost its taillights, but if you look hard enough, you might unearth another pair hiding in the back. The Country Sedan was the mid-trim station wagon that year, falling between the basic Ranch Wagon and the luxurious Country Squire. It was offered with a choice of six-cylinder or V-8 engine.

As you may be able to guess from the distinctive rock coloring in the background, the car was found in southeast Utah, just a few miles away from the stunning Arches National Park. It's one of the older cars I discovered at Bert's Auto Supply in Moab. I just learned this yard is about to close—but what about the fate of the cars?

Above: Hidden under a thick layer of Texas dust is a rust-free 1963 Galaxie. The car was found at Snyder Brothers Garage & Auto Wrecking in Whitney, Texas, where it acts as part of the yard's boundary fence. A steady stream of traffic on the unpaved road ensures that all the cars on the perimeter are always this color.

The yard has been at its present location for the better part of four decades, and some of the stock dates back to the early 1920s. While you'll find plenty of other old Fords on site, the yard actually specializes in Nash vehicles.

Left: You would normally struggle to find one decent 1963 Galaxie to scavenge for parts, but visitors to this Minnesota yard are spoiled. The car on the left is a standard Galaxie, while the one on the right has six hash marks in front of the taillight, indicating that it is a 500 model. The standard Galaxie is the more unusual of the two vehicles, as the four-door sedan derivative had just more than 82,000 buyers. The Galaxie 500, which cost an extra $160, achieved sales of nearly 206,000.

These cars were found in Windy Hill Auto Parts, a yard that has recently crushed thousands of aging vehicles. This pair was once part of an entire row of similarly aged Fords, but the rest have since met their maker. Just why these two were pardoned while so many others ended their days in the jaws of the crusher is a mystery.

Above: Rachel, Nevada, located on the world's only "extraterrestrial highway" (Highway 375), is home to about one hundred folks and goodness knows how many aliens. The town, which boasts a drinking establishment called the Little A'Le'Inn, is, as you might have guessed, the closest settlement to Nevada's infamous Area 51.

Rachel has dubbed itself the "UFO Capital of the World" and as such attracts UFO spotters from all corners of the globe. Do you reckon this unidentified flying Ford that I found hovering in a resident's garden has ever fooled any of them? There was nobody at home, but according to a neighbor, the car has been on blocks for quite some time.

Left, both: Junkyards are sometimes referred to as car cemeteries, but this is ridiculous. This Ford station wagon, photographed in the late 1990s in southern Kansas, has rather unusual cargo—it's packed full of bones. I would hope that we are looking at animal bones, but then again who knows? I remember that the junkyard dog looked particularly fierce—and come to think of it there was a sign warning that trespassers could be eaten.

Above: This Country Squire station wagon may have parted with its 289-cubic-inch, 195-horsepower V-8, but it still has plenty of parts to share with other 1964 Ford owners, including all that wood paneling. This car would have had the same level of trim as the Galaxie 500 XL, which included bucket seats and a floor-mounted transmission shifter.

Ford made nearly 47,000 Country Squires that year, with an almost equal split between six- and nine-passenger models. This is one of several similarly aged Fords I found in a junkyard in central Texas, a few miles away from Interstate 35.

Right: The 1970 Ford station wagon pictured must have been scrapped at an early age to have a trunk this thick growing out of its engine bay. I'm no horticulturalist, but that tree has got to be twenty years old. Needless to say, this wagon isn't the world's most desirable car, and the best it can hope for is to donate a few bits of trim before it is dragged from this spot to feed the insatiable appetite of the crusher.

The car was found in the Tennessee undergrowth, where it becomes more and more camouflaged by the day.

Below: At some point this rust-free 1970 Ford Torino fastback migrated north from Florida to Ohio. The exhaustive trip appears to have taken its toll on the car, which now awaits its fate in a junkyard just outside Cleveland.

The 1970 Torino, which was lower, longer, and wider than its predecessors, featured the popular option of flip-style hideaway headlights. That year also saw the introduction of the 351 Cleveland engines and the 429 Thunder Jet, Cobra Jet, and Super Cobra Jet engine options. Yet chances are that this Torino has a less exciting six-cylinder under its hood.

Above: The Edsel may be widely considered the biggest automotive flop of the twentieth century, but the make seems to have the same survival instincts as the cockroach. Examples are still turning up in salvage yards, and I could have dedicated a number of pages to them.

This one, photographed in 2003 in Bradford, Arkansas, is a 1959 Ranger two-door hardtop coupe. Although only 5,474 of them rolled off the Louisville production line, they were still the third-best sellers in the ten-strong model lineup that year.

When the Edsel was discontinued in November 1959, a grand total of 110,847 had found customers.

Below: An ultra-rare 1958 Edsel Bermuda, complete with distinctive fake wooden trim, is parked just a stone's throw away from Interstate 35 in central Texas. It's in the grounds of a body repair shop and will presumably one day get the restoration it so badly deserves.

There were three station wagons in the Edsel lineup in its first year of production: the Bermuda; the two-door, six-seat Roundup; and the four-door, six- or nine-seat Villager. At $3,155, the Bermuda was the most expensive of the bunch, and with just 892 registrations, it was the slowest seller. Like all Edsel station wagons, it had a 352-cubic-inch Ford V-8 under its hood.

Below: Welcome to Texas Exports, Little Valley Auto Ranch—where you'll find this intimate pair. You can't help but notice this place from the highway—they've parked about two dozen potential project cars out front in order to grab your attention. The view is just as good inside the yard, with roughly five hundred vintage parts cars to pick over.

On the bottom is a 1958 Mercury Commuter four-door station wagon, which easily supports the weight of the 1959 Edsel Ranger perched on its roof—then again this Edsel is only half the car it used to be. The red car on the right is yet another Edsel, one of 5,474 Ranger two-door hardtops that were built.

This rare 1959 Edsel Villager is part of an amazing collection of similarly aged classics I stumbled upon while traveling though Illinois in 2004.

The salvage yard, part of the Ace Auto Salvage empire, is a bit different from the norm. It is only open for a few hours on a Sunday morning. I was extremely fortunate to be there at the right time and was granted permission by owner Mitch Urban to wander around the secluded site for a few hours. The yard must have closed its doors to new vehicles about two decades ago and is now overrun with vegetation. Anyone wanting to buy a complete car would certainly need to come equipped with a weed whacker and chain saw.

Fewer than 8,000 Villagers were built in 1959, and you'll go a long time before you'll see another in a salvage yard. This one seems to have lost its roof a number of years ago and, as a result, the interior is virtually nonexistent.

My money is on this being a Mercury Coupe dating back to between 1949 and 1951, but I could be wrong. After all, there really isn't a lot to go by, and unlike the Tokheim gas pump in the foreground, it doesn't hold much value. The photograph was taken in southern Idaho, in the late 1990s. Since then the price of old pumps has rocketed, and examples of this age and vintage are regularly seen on Internet auction sites, where they fetch figures in excess of one thousand dollars.

You wouldn't think it would be very easy to hide ten thousand elderly cars, but I spent hours trying to locate Watts Repair Salvage & Auto in Wymore, Nebraska. When I finally did hit the correct dirt road and spotted an entire hillside full of cars, I realized it had been worth the effort.

You are looking at a Mercury Montclair, but you wouldn't necessarily know it from this angle. The car's only distinguishing front-end feature was its chrome headlight surrounds, and these are long-gone.

Model year 1958 was not a good one for the Big M, with production falling to 153,000. It finished the year as America's ninth-best-selling make, falling one place from the previous year.

The middle of nowhere Nevada is where you'll find this and many thousands of other unloved automotive relics from a bygone era. A lack of salvage yards in this sparsely populated state means people simply abandon their old vehicles out in the desert, where they are quickly forgotten. A lack of moisture keeps rust at bay, and it's not uncommon to see bullet-ridden remains from the 1920s basking in the hot desert sun.

Judging by the pattern of the missing side trim, this is, or at least was, a 1951 Lincoln four-door sedan. The entire front end, which at some point was detached from the rest of the car, can be found a couple of hundred yards from where I shot this photo.

Left: I am at a loss to understand how this near-immaculate Mercury ended up in an Idaho salvage yard. You are, of course, looking at a 1959 Monterey four-door sedan, which would be more at home in a classic car show than in this place. Not only are the bodywork and chrome incredibly straight, but so is the interior. However, it's unlikely to remain that way for long, with the driver's window open to the elements.

The 1959 Monterey was bigger than ever and arguably more attractive than its 1958 predecessor. This entry-level model came equipped with a 312-cubic-inch V-8 that gave the 4,140-pound giant a top speed of just under one hundred miles per hour.

Some states are better than others for hunting tin. I have learned to avoid the entire Northeast, with its salted highways. There, you are fortunate to find a vehicle manufactured before 1980 in a junkyard. You can forget most of Florida, too; the majority of its yards have been well picked over and a thriving tourist industry seems to prevent cars from being dumped just anywhere. The best salvage yards seem to be in the northern Midwest, particularly Minnesota and the Dakotas, while Nevada is definitely the best hunting ground for ownerless, bullet-ridden, prewar wrecks.

However, for sheer numbers of abandoned cars, seemingly discarded by the roadside where they stopped working, you can't beat New Mexico. Perhaps the state has since cleaned up its act, but when I was last traveling through I made slow progress, having to stop every few miles to take yet another photograph. This 1960 Mercury Comet, found on waste ground near Roswell, is a great example. The six-cylinder engine propelled the car to a top speed of just seventy-nine miles per hour; it made sixty miles per hour in a lethargic twenty-one seconds.

Above: I turned up at Winnick's Auto Sales & Parts of Shamokin, Pennsylvania, in the late 1990s expecting to find an incredible collection of aging metal. After all, the yard opened in the late 1930s and I was told it still had plenty of cars dating back to that era. However, as is often the case, I arrived a few months too late, having been beaten by the crusher. The yard's stocks were severely depleted and just a handful of classics survived. For some reason this Mercury Cougar was spared, whereas the remains of an old Cord apparently were not.

The Cougar was a Mustang in disguise, just two hundred pounds heavier and 6.7 inches longer, with disappearing headlights. It was also $350 more expensive than its sibling, which helped ensure that sales were never as strong. Judging by the presence of side-marker lights, this one dates back to 1968, the model's second year of production.

At the time of the photograph, the car had been off the road for some thirteen years.

Right: It's another Mercury, but this one is a rare Colony Park.

Although Minnesota's Windy Hill Auto Parts still has a couple thousand highly desirable old cars on site, the yard is just a shadow of its former self. In recent years, it has crushed several thousand cars, leaving acres of empty space in their wake. Not too long ago you would have seen several hundred other cars in this picture, but not any more. This 1958 Mercury, one of only 4,474 built, has the word "sold" scribbled in the back window, so presumably now has a new owner.

There were three station wagons in the Mercury stable in 1958: the Commuter, which shared the same trim as the Monterey, and the Voyager and Colony Park, which were both basically the same as the Montclair. Although available only in six-passenger guise, the Colony Park was still the most expensive in the lineup, with a $3,775 price tag.

Left: This appears to be a 1946 Lincoln, although there really weren't that many styling differences between the 1946, 1947, and 1948 model years. They all had a 305-cubic-inch V-12 under the hood. Lincoln produced 16,645 cars in 1946, which put it in sixteenth position, behind Studebaker and ahead of Crosley. It would fall to eighteenth in 1947 and nineteenth a year later.

The car is at one of the country's better-known salvage yards: L&L Classic Auto of Wendell, Idaho. More than ten thousand vehicles, from the 1920s, have made their home here. A good thousand or so appear to be ideal project cars.

Below: This is what the 1951 Lincoln looked like from the front. It was very similar to the 1950, but appeared to be in need of an emergency trip to the dentist. The center bar is much shorter than in the previous year, so consequently the car looks like it's missing a number of teeth. In fact, a trip to the optician wouldn't be such a bad idea for this one.

Other than its distinctive inset headlights and one rear suicide door, the bodywork is pretty much complete. Its condition might explain why this vehicle was saved while many of the cars that were once around it have been crushed.

Above: There are no shortages of people on the lookout for suicide-door Lincolns, so it's unusual to find them languishing in salvage yards. The 1964 Continental came with a $6,292 price tag, which was roughly the same price as three Ford Customs. Continental buyers were treated to a number of luxuries as standard, including power windows, power seats, and power steering.

This one was spotted some years ago in Elderly Auto Parts of Jasper, Oregon. What this small yard lacks in quantity it more than makes up for in quality. I found a number of seriously tempting restoration projects, including a 1958 two-door Edsel Ranger.

Left: In 1957, Lincoln produced one of its finest cars—the beautiful, luxurious, and astonishingly well-built Continental MkII—and then a year later along came this! The 1958 MkIII was nothing like its predecessor and represented a huge downgrade. However, because it now shared the same basic body as a regular Lincoln, it was considerably cheaper to build, allowing the company to slash the asking price by some $4,000. As a result, more than 12,000 MkIIIs found buyers in 1958, compared with only 446 of the stunning MkIIs.

This is a two-door hardtop coupe, one of just 2,328 to find a buyer. At first glance, it appears that this is one of the 2 percent of Lincolns that came with air suspension, but a closer look reveals that its wheels have simply sunk into the ground. It is a resident of Car Connection in Texas.

CHAPTER 2

CHRYSLER

"Square noses, round noses, rusty noses, shovel noses, and the long curves of streamlines, and the flat surfaces before streamlining. Bargains today."
—*John Steinbeck, The Grapes of Wrath*

A 1938 Chrysler hides in the foliage in one of Illinois' best junkyards. Actually, Ace Auto Salvage has several sites around the northern part of the state, and proprietor Mitch Urban was kind enough to give me a guided tour of all of them—including several barns filled with his private collection.

This particular site was on the verge of closing in 2005 and Mitch was in the process of clearing out the stock. While some cars were being crushed, rare vehicles like this Chrysler were to be transferred to another site.

I found this trio of Mopars basking in the spring sunshine beside a Minnesota roadside. From left to right are a 1959 Plymouth Fury, a 1956 Chrysler convertible, and a 1955 Chrysler New Yorker Deluxe.

It's difficult to tell from this angle whether the middle car is a genuine convertible, but if it is, it's an extremely rare beast. Fewer than 2,000 convertibles were built that year across the model range. Then again, someone may have simply taken a hacksaw to the roof of a two-door sedan—it certainly wouldn't have been the first time.

Left: You don't find many 1920s cars in salvage yards these days, especially not in such wonderful condition. Those that still do surface, like this Chrysler, are invariably found in Arizona, where the warm climate is perfect for prolonging the life of old classics. This car appears to be a 1928 C52 coupe, which at $670 was the cheapest car in the Chrysler model lineup. That was a good year for Chrysler, as it produced a record 160,670 automobiles. It would be another twenty-two years before that figure was exceeded.

Below: I immediately recognized this as a 1926 Chrysler—just as soon as I had read the yellow identification on the side of the car. This eighty-year-old vehicle was one of the oldest at Wiseman's Auto Salvage in Casa Grande, Arizona. This photograph was taken in about 2001, at which point the yard had around three thousand cars dating from the 1920s to the 1970s. I have since learned that shortly after my visit, proprietor Ron Wiseman was tragically killed in a car accident. The yard is still open today, but is being run by Phoenix-based Desert Valley Auto Parts.

   This Chrysler is doing pretty well for its age, and although it has parted company with its six-cylinder engine, it has managed to regain its glass, sun visor, side lights, and all four of its wooden wheels.

Above: There must be a shortage of game in southern Idaho or else an extremely shortsighted hunter mistook this 1941 Chrysler for an elk. How else do you explain all the shattered windows and the fact that the doors are riddled with bullet holes? In this dilapidated state, a restoration would be an ambitious undertaking.

The car is residing at Vintage Automotive in Mountain Home, Idaho, one of the town's two amazing salvage yards. Despite the yard being closed for the evening, owner Jim Hines let me wander the place as long as the daylight permitted.

Right: By counting the vertical bars on the waterfall grille, you can determine that this Chrysler Airflow is a 1934 model. Complete with its recessed headlights and alligator-style hood, the Carl Breer–designed Airflow was the shape of things to come. Its aerodynamic styling was leagues ahead of the competition and came about with the help of wind tunnels and the advice of aviation pioneer Orville Wright. The streamlined design helped the car to achieve a top speed of eighty-eight miles per hour and a zero-to-sixty miles per hour time of just less than twenty seconds.

Although the Airflow had an amazing ability to turn heads, it didn't have the same success at opening wallets. The car was not a sales success and was discontinued in 1937.

Left: How's this for an idyllic scene—a 1940 Chrysler overlooking one of Minnesota's ten thousand lakes? At least I think it's a 1940 model. The problem is that the main external differences between the 1939 and 1940 Chryslers are recessed, sealed-beam headlamps (which you can't see) and more massive fenders (which in this case don't appear to be the shape that Chrysler originally intended). Some 100,000 customers became proud Chrysler owners in 1940, which was enough to make the marque America's ninth largest car producer that year.

But Walter P. Chrysler wasn't around to see it because he died that August, at age sixty-five, of a cerebral hemorrhage.

Below: Although only a couple of hundred people live in Goldfield, Nevada, today, this town was once over-flowing with prospectors looking for gold. At the beginning of the last century, Goldfield was home to as many as thirty thousand residents. In fact, some ninety million dollars of high-grade gold ore was mined in the surrounding area between 1904 and 1960.

But the gold ran out and so did the people. There have since been a series of fires and floods, and today much of the town has reverted back to desert. It does still have some incredible old buildings, which like this Chrysler, dating between 1946 and 1948, will hopefully be restored one day.

Above: Decatur, Texas, about thirty miles north of Fort Worth, is where this once proud 1955 Chrysler can be found. At least that's where it was in 2003 when I passed by.

I know absolutely nothing about the history or the future of this car. A lady working at a nearby gas station gave me permission to take the photograph, but she had no idea who the car belonged to.

And if ever you find yourself in this part of the world, be sure to check out the town's petrified wood gas station. It has to be one of a kind.

Left: Chrysler did make a woody in 1949, but it didn't look like this. I've photographed plenty of cars with trees growing through them, but this is the only one I've ever found with a tree lying on top of it. The car's roof is holding up pretty well considering the weight it's been burdened with, and judging by the way the wood is rotting, the roof probably has been supporting it for a number of years.

The car is a 1949 Chrysler Windsor, complete with the special-edition Highlander-plaid interior.

Above: I'm not sure why someone painted a misleading "53" on the back of a rare 1956 Chrysler Windsor convertible. The car's ragtop is in tatters, which means the interior will soon be a terrible mess, too. But of more importance to any potential restorer is exactly why the car has snapped in half. It doesn't appear to be a corrosion problem—the bodywork is still relatively sound.

Were it not in such appalling condition, the convertible would surely have been rescued by now. After all, just 1,011 of these found buyers in 1956, making them as rare as rocking-horse manure. In fact, fully restored examples can fetch as much as $30,000 these days.

Right: The entire 1934 DeSoto lineup featured Chrysler's new, and highly advanced, Airflow design, which included a distinctive grille, rear fender skirts, and a hood that extended beyond the front bumper. The car was equipped with a six-cylinder engine, which, thanks to the aerodynamic design, was capable of reaching twenty-two miles per gallon. At $995, the DeSoto was $350 cheaper than its Chrysler sibling and outsold it by almost 3,000 units. This photo is of the four-door sedan, which was the most popular derivative and achieved 11,713 registrations.

Just imagine how much cash you could throw at this bottomless pit to coax it back onto the highway. Still, if you are either brave, stupid, or both, get on the phone to Kelly's Auto Salvage of Arlee, Montana.

Left: I wouldn't even guess as to the exact year this wooden-wheeled DeSoto was manufactured, but it is certainly a very early model. The DeSoto brand first emerged in 1929 and was priced at $845 to compete with Chrysler and Plymouth offerings. Although Dodge was already doing a good job of plugging the gap, this didn't affect the new arrival's success. The DeSoto had a truly phenomenal first year, achieving more than 81,000 sales. Although DeSoto set a first year sales record, its popularity went largely downhill after that.

The name, of course, would soldier on until the end of 1960. Having survived for so long, surely the DeSoto deserves to be rescued from this Idaho yard.

Row F of this Pennsylvania yard is home to a 1938 DeSoto four-door sedan. Fortunately for the DeSoto, the junkyard dog also lives in Row F. Not only has the vehicle survived the crusher, but thanks to its canine guard, nobody's even dared remove a part during the decade it has stood in this spot.

When I first got on my hands and knees to take this picture, I hadn't actually noticed the kennel. Without warning, the dog emerged and then made a beeline for me. I scrambled to my feet, thinking of the "sic balls" junkyard dog in the movie *Stand By Me*, but there was no time to run. Just inches away from me, the dog's chain tightened, and, in true cartoon-fashion, he did an acrobatic back flip and landed on his feet, snarling.

Below: A 1956 DeSoto Firedome turns its back on the barbaric events that are unfolding behind it. Then again, it's only a 1980s Buick Century that is being eaten by the crusher.

With so much clean sheet metal on offer, the DeSoto is safe for the time being. But as it is gradually stripped of parts, it edges ever closer to the crusher. A few cosmetic items have already been scrounged, and it won't be long until the bigger items start to disappear.

This photograph was taken in a salvage yard in Fairbury, Nebraska.

Above: When I last paid a visit to Larry's Auto Salvage of Las Vegas, the yard had more than five hundred cars, the majority of which were pre-1970s models and a handful were 1940s relics. However, I went back in 2006 and discovered the yard was gone—replaced by a garden center. While some of the cars were bought by other salvage yards, the majority apparently were sent straight to the crusher.

I wonder what happened to this 1952 DeSoto Custom Sportsman two-door hardtop coupe. Considering its rust-free condition and the fact that fewer than 9,000 were built, I hope it was one of the lucky few that found new homes.

Left: Can you help this homeless four-door 1957 DeSoto Sportsman? It is gradually being engulfed by the forest in a far-flung forgotten corner of a Minnesota junkyard. The car has clearly been neglected for a number of years. Potential rescuers will first have to clear a path through these fast-growing trees to reach the forgotten relic, then they will face a tough restoration.

Although rust is gradually eating away the front fenders, the doors and trunk lid are remarkably corrosion free. The chrome is close to perfect, too, and I'm surprised it hasn't been removed yet.

DeSotos manufactured in 1957 featured all-new styling and were significantly longer and lower than the previous year. These, according to many people, were the best-looking DeSotos. Attractive or not, the marque only managed to take a 1.63 percent share of the total market that year.

Above: It is amazing how many Dodge Brothers cars still turn up—a tribute to the build quality and the sheer numbers that were built. Having spent hours with my head in reference books and days e-mailing copies of this picture to numerous car spotters, I have come to the decision that this vehicle is a 1925 model.

What is certain, though, is its location—the uniquely named town of Nothing, Arizona. Nothing, population four, can be found on Highway 93 between Wickenburg and Kingman. The town may have changed now, but when I was there in the late 1990s, it was certainly living up to its name. It was home to a makeshift shop, a gas station, a handful of abandoned cars, and nothing else.

Right: I only hope that I'm looking as good as this 1924 Dodge DB coupe when I'm eighty-two years old. While neither the roof nor the interior is in a particularly good condition, check out all that rust-free and remarkably straight sheet metal. Although it looks like there's a layer of frost sitting on the trunk, this is south Texas in late summer, and that's dust from a nearby unpaved road.

Although I've put this picture in the Chrysler chapter, Dodge Brothers was an independent company for most of the 1920s. It was purchased in 1928 by Walter P. Chrysler for $170 million.

Below: This barefoot orphan is a Dodge Brothers four-door sedan. One of the employees at Windy Hill Auto Parts, where the car resides, believes it to be a 1925 model, and I'm certainly not going to argue. I find cars from this era such a challenge to identify, and indeed, the only notable difference between the 1924 and 1925 Dodge was the one-piece windshield on the later cars. That really doesn't help in identifying this one.

The car's inline four-cylinder engine, which was good for 35 horsepower, is long gone, as are all remnants of the interior.

Why hasn't someone removed this Dodge's front bumper overriders yet? They were an optional item in 1941, and there must be a demand for them today. Come to think of it, that distinctive heart-shaped grille is in particularly nice condition, too.

The 1941 production year marked a significant milestone for Dodge—the manufacturer sold its five millionth car after twenty-seven years in existence. Actual production that year was 237,002 units, which was enough to rank Dodge as America's seventh-best-selling make.

This was also the year that the Fluid Drive transmission was finally offered to Dodge buyers. Previously, it was only available on Chrysler and DeSoto products. It cost an additional $25.

The future looks bleak for this 1938 Dodge, a shadow of its former self. It's unlikely to yield many more parts and is sure to die in the crusher before very long. Once upon a time, it was a two-door sedan, but not any more. The roof must have been removed many years ago—after all, just look at what state the interior is in. It takes a good few years for seats to rot down to bare metal.

Above: It's one of life's little mysteries why this highly desirable Dodge convertible ended up in this state. Ragtops always cost a little more than their roofed siblings, and with time the price gap tends to widen. When this vehicle was sitting in the showroom, its price tag was about $400 more than that of the equivalent four-door sedan. Yet today, in pristine condition, it would fetch an additional $15,000. Obviously it's not worth much in this dismal state, but it should be saved nonetheless.

From this angle, it's difficult to tell whether this is a 1949 or a 1950 Coronet, as the grilles were the main differentiating feature between the two years. Either way, it is an incredibly rare car, with just 2,411 or 1,800 examples being built, respectively.

Although this Coronet would need a lot of work to get it back on the road, the finished result would surely be worth it.

Right: In 1957, the Coronet looked like a very different vehicle. It was longer, lower, and wider than before, and it featured recessed headlights and eyebrows. It was widely considered to be one of the best-looking cars of the year—although you wouldn't think so by looking at this one. These vehicles not only looked great, but they shifted great, too. Even the standard V-8 was a quick mover, achieving sixty miles per hour in ten seconds. Then there was the awesome D500 Hemi, which was more than capable of leaving smoking rubber on the tarmac.

This one, photographed in a Spokane, Washington, yard, has had its engine replaced by a more environmentally friendly tree.

Below: A lonely 1956 Dodge thaws out in the spring sunshine after another hard Utah winter.

It's a Coronet and a severely vandalized one at that. All but one window has been smashed and even the lights have had a good kicking. The 1956 Coronets were very similar to the successful 1955 models, but they had the addition of a more prominent tailfin.

In its quest for more power, Dodge offered its cars with as much as 295 horsepower in 1956, but being the entry-level car, this one would more than likely have had a six-cylinder engine under its hood.

It was actually a local policeman who pointed me in the direction of this wreck.

Right: Dodge sales took a nosedive in 1958, a consequence of a nationwide recession and the manufacturer's growing reputation for poor build quality. One of the problems was premature corrosion, although I'm guessing that this one didn't look as bad in the late 1950s as it does now. This is a Dodge Royal Lancer two-door hardtop, identified by the pair of chrome hood ornaments. Only 15,500 Royals were built in 1958, and that figure covers all three body styles.

I always photograph the cars exactly how I find them, and if the hood, doors, trunk, or windows are open, then that's how they remain. The car was located about one hundred miles south of Chicago.

Below: Dodge 440 station wagons from 1964 are few and far between in salvage yards, and you certainly don't find many like this one in such great condition. It may have waved goodbye to its V-8, but other than that, it appears to be complete. It wouldn't cost a fortune to get it back on the road. Judging by the writing on the doors, the wagon once belonged to a Hall Refrigeration engineer. It was found at Kelley's Auto Salvage in Arlee, Montana.

No prizes for guessing that this photograph was taken in Mountain Home, Idaho, at Vintage Automotive. This Dodge Dart Seneca dates back to 1960. Although the model would soon evolve into a proper compact, it was no more than a small full-size car in its first year. In fact, it was just four inches shorter than its larger stable mates. The Seneca was the cheapest offering, followed by the Pioneer and the Phoenix.

The driver's door on this vehicle has been used as target practice, but there is still plenty more clean sheet metal, including an immaculate trunk lid. A lack of glass hasn't done the interior any favors, though.

Right: Would you do this to a Dodge Charger fastback coupe? Personally, I think the culprit should be strung up for committing such a crime! When I asked the owner of the Ohio yard if he knew anything of the car's history, he shook his head and said, "Around these parts, if it can't pull a plow, then it ain't worth having."

Fastback styling was all the rage in the mid-1960s, and this was Dodge's version of it. The lack of fender-mounted turn signals leads me to believe that this coupe is a 1966 model.

Below: These distinctive fender-mounted taillights more than made up for any inadequacies the 1956 Imperial may have had in the tailfin department. Despite weighing more than 4,500 pounds, the V-8 in this four-door sedan would still have been good for over 100 miles per hour. Fewer than 7,000 Imperials were built, all equipped with a host of luxuries, including four-way power seats and power steering. You had to pay extra if you wanted power windows or air conditioning.

This one, which has clearly been laid up for a few years, was photographed beside what appears to be a derelict house in Tennessee. A neighbor told me the owner was currently out of town and said he wouldn't mind me taking the photograph if I didn't reveal its exact location.

Searching for abandoned cars can be a dangerous business. Over the years, I've been mauled by junkyard dogs, attacked by poison ivy, had close encounters with rattlers and scorpions, and even knelt on a nest of fire ants. But this is the only time I've come close to being stung by a bee!

Every muscle-car fan dreams of finding one of these in a hedgerow—a 1969 Dodge Coronet Super Bee. What can I say about this car that you don't already know? Well, it was found in the far corner of a Tennessee salvage yard, where it is being slowly engulfed by foliage. Although still salvageable and relatively rust free, this car would take a lot of time and money to get it back on the road. A good place to start would be tracking down a new back seat, as the current one is clearly beyond help.

Below: This 1963 Imperial Crown four-door hardtop resides in H. L. Hodges Salvage Yard & Used Parts in Monroe, Georgia—along with half the area's old school buses. At over $5,500, the Cadillac competitor was an expensive car. In fact, you could have bought yourself no less than three Dodge D100 pickups for the same money. I can't imagine that too many were sold in rural Georgia, and my guess is that this one hailed from nearby Atlanta.

Although it has stood in this spot for a number of years, it remains relatively intact. Had it been a pickup truck or a more commonly seen car, the vehicle would probably have a different history, being stripped of most salvageable parts within a year or two of arriving here.

Above: Over the years, a huge number of early 1960s Imperials have ended their days in the hands of demolition-derby drivers, a tribute to the immense strength of their rigid frame construction. However, their indestructibility means that they are now outlawed at the majority of competitions, thus increasing the survival rates for cars like this.

This is a 1962 pillarless hardtop sedan, complete with space-age square steering wheel. It is part of a private collection of classic cars I found in Jasper, Oregon. Of the 14,337 Imperials sold in 1962, roughly half were these sedans.

Left: This seriously vandalized 1964 Imperial Custom Coupe stood out like a sore thumb in a field full of automotive junk a few miles north of Pratt, Kansas. It is a rare find, considering just over 5,000 were built, and it's a crying shame that someone has decided to put bricks through each of its windows and lights. I guess there can't be too much to do in the evenings in this part of Kansas.

The picture was taken in 1997, and when I returned a year later the field was completely empty. Was the vehicle crushed, or is it alive and well in someone's garage? Surely the abundance of clean sheet metal would have increased its chances of survival.

Above: Imperial Crown two-door hardtops manufactured in 1966 are rare, especially in such clean condition. It won't take a genius to guess this one was found out west—in Las Vegas, Nevada, to be exact. The favorable climate attracts tin hunters from all over the world to the Silver State, and after seeing so little rust on a forty-year-old car, you can understand why. Then again, this car's condition may also have something to do with the seven rust-preventing dips and sprays that all 1966 Imperials were treated to at the factory.

Despite the addition of a 440-cubic-inch V-8, which replaced the previous year's 413-cubic-inch version, the Imperial's selling price dropped by $50 in 1966. However, the price reduction was enough to entice only 2,373 buyers to part with their cash.

The 1966 model in this photo was in another yard that, unfortunately, no longer exists.

Above: Plymouth did a fantastic job of disguising that its 1939 cars used the same basic body as the 1937 and 1938 models. The windshield and the roof panel were both changed, but the most radical alteration was the front end. By mounting the headlamps in the fenders, the car took on a completely different appearance. This two-door version has lost its 82 horsepower six-cylinder engine, but it is doing a lot better than the anonymous disheveled wreck in the background.

Montana is my favorite state for hunting tin, as it seems to have the largest number of salvage yards concentrating on vintage vehicles. Elsewhere, cars from this era would have been lost to the crusher decades ago.

Left: The car nearest the camera is a 1937 Plymouth, and a 1940 Pontiac is next to it.

The year 1937 was a bit of a milestone for Plymouth, as the manufacturer's two millionth car rolled off the production line. It was sold to the same customer who had bought both the first and the one-millionth models. The same buyer would get the opportunity to purchase the three-millionth just two years later.

The most exciting thing to happen to the Pontiac offerings in 1940 was the introduction of sealed beam headlights and adjustable seats—neither of which survive on this example. And check out that agricultural-type bumper. It definitely didn't leave the factory with that.

Both cars are residents of a salvage yard in Wendell, Idaho, and are typical of the huge number of rust-free restoration projects waiting for some TLC.

Above: There are certain rules you need to follow when trying to locate abandoned cars—the most important being that you should avoid big towns and cities in favor of small rural communities. It is here, well off the beaten track, that you are most likely to find those forgotten treasures. Whenever I arrive anywhere, I turn off Main Street as quickly as possible and skirt around the edges of the town instead. If there are any old cars to be found, they'll be here.

Another option is to ask around because you can't beat local knowledge. That's exactly how I found this Plymouth. I was chatting to the owner of a gas station on the Oklahoma-Texas border when a lady behind me announced that I could photograph the old cars on her ranch. Having followed her pickup through several hundred acres of fields and done some serious damage to the underside of my rental car, I came upon this vehicle. She said it was a 1948 two-door sedan, which sounds about right.

Right: I'm not too sure what the purpose of the "41" in the windshield is, because this car certainly isn't a 1941 Plymouth. Having said that, I can't be too sure exactly what year this vehicle hails from, as this design was kept throughout 1946, 1947, 1948, and even the first few months of 1949.

Note that the hood has been removed at some point and is now just resting in its former position. That tells me that the 95 horsepower, 218-cubic-inch six-cylinder engine has found a new home. Yet this is still a solid car, and restoration certainly isn't out of the question.

The car is currently residing in Bradford, Arkansas.

Left: The 1940 Plymouth was hailed as "the low priced beauty with the luxury ride," but "beauty" and "luxury" are not words that spring to mind when looking at such a wreck. Although the 1940 models looked rather similar to the previous year's, they featured an all-new body. In fact, Plymouth proudly proclaimed that the only interchangeable piece of sheet metal between the two years was the sailing-ship hood ornament, one of the few parts that this one has managed to keep hold of.

That year Plymouth reached 423,155 sales, which was enough for third position in the industry. It was the closest the manufacturer would ever get to finishing above Ford.

Top: There's no shortage of old cars, including this 1955 Plymouth Plaza, sitting by roadsides in northern Washington and Montana. The Plaza was the cheapest offering that year and didn't have as much chrome as its more expensive siblings. The 1955 Plymouths, with their "Forward Look" design, were an instant success. They were significantly sleeker than the company's stodgy offerings the previous year and sold well.

Bottom: This Texas yard has a lot of Mopars on site, including a tired 1958 Custom Suburban station wagon. Of course, the most desirable of all the 1958 Plymouths is the Fury, thanks to its starring role in the Stephen King book and John Carpenter film *Christine*. Almost two dozen fully restored examples were used during the making of the film (including a handful of Belvederes and Savoys in disguise) and about sixteen of them were destroyed. Clearly not all 1958 Plymouths have the ability to repair themselves.

California's numerous tourist attractions pull in visitors from all over the world, but I doubt if many end up in Coalinga. That is a pity really because I found plenty of things worth pointing a camera at. For instance, look at this hideously disfigured wreck, which I found on the outskirts of town. Despite its appalling condition, there's no mistaking that it's a two-door 1959 Plymouth Savoy. The Savoy, offered with a choice of six-cylinder or V-8 engine, was the entry-level car. Next most expensive was the Belvedere, followed by the Fury and Sport Fury.

Plymouth's eleven millionth vehicle rolled off the line in 1959.

Above: Although someone has stripped the car of its medallions and distinctive chrome trim, you can still tell this is a top-of-the-range 1959 Sport Fury two-door hardtop coupe. For $2,927, Sport Fury customers were treated to such delights as swivel front seats, which improved access for rear passengers when the door was open. The Sport Fury also had a trunk-lid tire-cover stamping, although this one is long gone. Best of all, though, Sport Fury owners had plenty of oomph beneath their right foot—at least if they opted for the 361-cubic-inch V-8 with its top speed of 110 miles per hour.

This car was photographed in an Arkansas yard, about sixty miles northeast of Little Rock.

Right: Plymouth Fury buyers were offered a choice of five specification levels in 1967—the Fury I, Fury II, Fury III, Sport Fury, and the Fury VIP. The four-door hardtop seen here is a middle-of-the-road Fury III, which was originally bought for $2,922. For their bucks, buyers got everything found in the lesser Fury II, plus a more luxurious interior and torsion-bar front suspension. Originally, this vehicle had the optional Commando V-8 engine under its hood.

Furys of this era, with their slab sides and Coke-bottle styling, proved a popular choice among police forces across the United States.

Below: Tara Springs Autos in Arizona is home to a pair of intimate Mopars. You don't have to be a genius to recognize that the top car is an original Plymouth Barracuda. Its massive rear window would have made a great hatchback, but it wasn't to be. Instead, the car's designers gave it a conventional trunk lid, and although the rear seats could be folded down to reveal a large amount of storage space, access was limited.

It is unusual to find a 'Cuda with an intact rear window, and this one appears to be safely out of harm's way, sitting comfortably on the roof of a 1974 Plymouth Satellite Sebring.

Below: When I spotted this Plymouth Fury, the eerie noise made by the wind opening and closing the trunk lid could be heard throughout the yard. It was almost like a cry for attention, like a dog in a kennel whining at potential new owners, hoping to be rescued by a loving family. Unfortunately, the vehicle's cries are falling on deaf ears, as it appears nobody is in the market for a 1973 Fury Gran Coupe two-door hardtop. Even more worrisome is the fact the Fury is parked next to a large pile of recently crushed vehicles, including several from the same era. Given its four-thousand-pound weight and the current sky-high price of scrap metal, I think it's living on borrowed time.

Above: The Plymouth Duster was introduced in 1970 as a replacement for the two-door Valiant sedan. The special edition Gold Duster came along halfway through the first year of production. Complete with dual horns, whitewalls, bucket seats, distinctive gold paint, transfers, and a choice of a 225-cubic-inch six-cylinder or a 318-cubic-inch V-8 engine, the Gold Duster was the one to own. During the Duster's six-year production run, it did for compact cars what its big brother, the Road Runner, did for intermediates.

This picture was taken in Cima, California, a tiny community right in the middle of the Mojave National Preserve. The car has been banished to what appears to be the town dump, and its days are clearly numbered. Judging by the bullet holes at the rear, it is good only for target practice today.

Left: Beep, beep. Does this car need any more of an introduction? Plymouth put a 335-horsepower, 383-cubic-inch V-8 engine into a Belvedere two-door sedan, gave it a cartoon name, then sat back and watched them fly out of the showrooms. The Road Runner moved pretty fast on the highway, too, hitting sixty miles per hour in just 7.1 seconds. And those fitted with the optional 425-horsepower, 426-cubic-inch Hemi could shave off another 1.8 seconds from that time.

This 1968 example was photographed in 2003 at a salvage yard in Black Canyon City, Arizona. Its bodywork appears to be relatively sound, and it still holds air in all four tires. Although the windscreen has been missing for a few years, the state's arid climate hasn't affected the interior that much. This Road Runner was for sale and must have found a new owner by now.

CHAPTER 3

❖

GENERAL MOTORS

"Dad called [General Motors designer] Harley Earl's designs 'chrome-plated barges.' . . . He said that, if left to his own devices, Harley Earl would put fins on a TV or refrigerator."
—Laurence Loewy, auto designer Raymond Loewy's daughter

When you have more than fifty acres of land, you can afford to spread out your stock a bit. That certainly seems to be the case for Tennessee-based Holt's Auto Salvage. When I visited the yard, more than three thousand cars were on site, but many were as isolated as this one. This is a 1956 Oldsmobile Holiday two-door hardtop, but I'm unable to determine whether it's the 88 or the plusher Super 88. The latter, which was the better seller of the two, featured internal luxuries such as foam-rubber seat cushions and front and rear carpeting. The only other telltale external difference between it and its sibling was a badge on the trunk lid.

Right: Not the easiest car to identify, not the easiest to find either. Its location came from a tip, from an elderly man who referred to himself as "FBI Eric." I met him at an Idaho diner. FBI Eric was a keen walker, and on his travels around the Idaho/Nevada border he apparently unearthed countless old abandoned wrecks. I chose to track this one down because it was the closest to the highway and getting to it only involved a one-mile walk along a stream.

FBI Eric told me this vehicle is a 1933 Buick, but then he also informed me that he's a close personal friend of the Queen of England and was an astronaut in the 1950s.

Below: This 1940 Buick is one of the most restorable cars at Vintage Automotive in Mountain Home, Idaho. These cars may have looked very different from the previous year's model, but they were basically the same. It's amazing what a revised grille, redesigned fenders, and new headlights will do for a car's appearance. Note the optional roof-mounted radio antenna on this 1940 model—a sign that the original owner opted for the $63 Sonomatic radio.

Buick and its parent company, General Motors, had milestone years in 1940, when they produced their four millionth and twenty-five millionth cars, respectively.

It may still have its big toothy grin, but what exactly does this bucktooth-mouthed Buick have to smile about? It's sitting in an Arkansas salvage yard, and, other than having a good set of fangs, it isn't exactly in the best of health. Although 1950 Buicks featured an all-new body, those ventiports were not a new addition. They started gracing the fenders of Buicks a year earlier and continued to do so for a long time. Roadmasters were treated to four of them, while this midrange Super four-door sedan and the lower-priced Special received three.

This Buick once sported a plush interior with cloth-finished seats. But with a lack of window glass, these seats and the rest of the interior have long since been ruined.

Above: Here's another Buick in serious need of a visit to the dentist. The car is a resident of Hopkins Antique Autos & Parts in Idaho, a yard that specializes in old, collectible autos. When I visited in the late 1990s, more than one thousand vehicles were on the fifteen-acre site. However, a good proportion of those were parts cars, with few as complete as this one.

While that carpet of pine needles may be aesthetically pleasing to the camera, it isn't doing the car any favors. By trapping in moisture, the needles will help attract the dreaded tin worm. This engineless car is a 1954 model.

Left, both: Nineteen fifty-two Buick Supers are supposed to have three large holes in each front fender, but not another hundred small holes in the rear fender and door. This car was found in Rachel, Nevada, near the Belted Mountain Range (pictured in the background). This is about as close as you can get to the mountains, though, as they belong to the U.S. government and trespassing is strictly prohibited. Somewhere behind these mountains is the infamous Groom Lake test facility, otherwise known as Dreamland or Area 51. Back in the 1950s, nuclear bomb testing was conducted on this massive military site, and the Buick looks as if it got caught up in one of the explosions.

Right: The brick that smashed this 1955 Buick Special Riviera's rear window is still sitting on the trunk lid, just waiting for vandals to return and finish off the job they started. The two-door coupe was the most popular of all the body styles that year, with a production run of 155,818 units. It was also one of the cheapest, with a $2,332 asking price.

The car pictured is in Danville, Kansas, parked next to a 1955 four-door Special. I took this photograph in the late 1990s.

Below: An Illinois hedgerow is home to this 1956 Buick Special Estate Wagon. Fewer than 14,000 of these were built, and they don't often turn up like this. This four-door wagon may not be in the best condition, but it still has an abundance of parts to offer, including a hard-to-find rear tailgate and window. It once had a 322-cubic-inch V-8 under its hood, powering the four-thousand-pound wagon to sixty miles per hour in just over eleven seconds. The only other Buick station wagon available that year was the Century, which had a few more luxuries and wore an all-important fourth ventiport on its fender.

Above: Rochester is not the prettiest town in the Silver State; in fact, it's downright ugly. But like so many of Nevada's long-since abandoned mining camps, it is great hunting ground for old automobiles. Between 1860 and 1913, this town's thriving population of around fifteen hundred helped mine ten million dollars of silver ore from these hills. But today, the only metal that can be pulled from the polluted ground is the scrap metal left here by the townsfolk a century ago and a handful of cars and empty cans of cyanide dumped by a few die-hard prospectors during the 1960s and 1970s.

Badly disfigured by falling rocks, this vehicle appears to be the pitiful remains of a 1957 Buick.

Below: Here's another ragged ragtop. It is one of the many collectible, but badly damaged cars at Ace Auto Salvage in Tonica, Illinois. It looks like the car ended up in this place following a substantial rear-end collision, but since then rust has become an equally serious problem. I'll be very surprised if it leaves the yard in one piece.

The car appears to be a 1967 Buick Skylark, identified by the simulated front fender vents and the lack of ventiports. While this model once had a 220-horsepower V-8, Buick also offered a high-performance GS400 convertible model, which was good for 340 horsepower.

Above: One of the workers in this Nevada salvage yard was happy for me to take photographs, but requested that I don't mention the yard's location. Although it doesn't concentrate on vintage tin, there are a number of oldies dotted around the place, including this 1966 Riviera. The model underwent a major restyling that year and featured all-new retractable headlights. It gained fastback styling, too, and the hood was substantially longer than before.

The interior also received a makeover, including the addition of a new instrument panel with drum-type speedometer. Luxury items included power steering, dual-speed windshield wipers, and carpeting throughout. Drivers were also impressed with the 340 horses under their feet, which equated to a 16.4-second quarter mile and a top speed of over 120 miles per hour. All in all, the car was a huge success, and sales were up by 50 percent over the previous year.

Left: The "boattail" Riviera is indisputably one of the best-looking American cars of the early 1970s. However, it's also safe to say that its best features were its unique roof, rear window, and sweeping side sculpture, none of which exist on this 1972 version. This vehicle looks like it has been decapitated by an eighteen-wheeler, like the car Sheriff Buford T. Justice drove in the closing scenes of the film *Smokey and the Bandit*.

It's good to see that someone bothered to wind up the driver's window—after all, winters can be hard in this part of Idaho.

Above: It appears that this Nebraska-based 1947 Cadillac has suffered from severe fire damage. Either that or it has spent a good portion of its life in a riverbed or somewhere similarly damp. A vast section of the rear roof has completely rotted away, and you can put your fingers through the holes in the rear door. Without having a grille to study, it's practically impossible to determine whether this four-door sedan is a 1946 or a 1947 example. One of the other minor differences between the two years was the word "Cadillac" on the front fenders, which changed from block lettering to script. Of course, the badge is missing here.

The safest bet is that this is a 1947 model because more than twice as many of these were built. For the second time, GM's luxury marque outsold rival Packard in 1947, a streak that would continue from 1950 on.

Right: The derelict foundation of a building in Goodsprings, Nevada, is home to this disheveled 1951 Cadillac Series 62 four-door sedan. Although most of the chrome trim and body panels remain intact, that impressive 331-cubic-inch V-8 is long gone.

This near ghost town was originally a wealthy community that produced lead, zinc, silver, and gold. By the early 1950s, the mines were all but exhausted, and the town was barely surviving. Then in 1952, prospectors struck gold once more, and Goodsprings underwent a mini revival. Perhaps a mine owner splurged on a one-year-old Cadillac to celebrate his newfound wealth—who knows?

Below: At some point, this 1959 Cadillac went up in flames, and despite the damage being restricted to the engine bay, it must have burned for a while for the hood to melt like this. Although this is the most instantly recognizable Cadillac of all time, it just doesn't look the same without those giant tailfins and twin bullet tail lamps. I wonder where they are now. The whole rear end is probably sitting in a 1950s-themed diner, converted into a seat.

I peered inside this car and was greeted by a lot of hissing and waving of clawed paws. The Illinois yard's resident cat had just produced a litter of kittens in the passenger footwell and didn't appreciate being disturbed. This was one cool cat; out of the hundreds of mundane American and Japanese cars on site, she chose the yard's one and only Cadillac to give birth in.

Below: The chances of a restoration are slim for a 1964 Cadillac DeVille two-door ragtop. Fewer than 18,000 customers were prepared to hand over $5,612 for one of these luxury convertibles when they were first built, and today they are highly collectible. Judging by the color of the trunk lid and roof framework, this car may also have suffered from fire damage. Maybe that explains why it's in a salvage yard and not safely hidden away in someone's garage. So is there a case of Cadillac pyromania going on, or is it just coincidence that four out of the five examples featured in this book were at one point smoking?

Note the saguaro cactus in the background, cluing you in that this picture was taken in Arizona at Tara Springs Autos.

Above: An arrow whizzed past my leg and lodged in the ground a few feet in front of me while I was taking this picture. I turned around, half expecting to find a renegade Sioux warrior about to attack, only to see a couple of kids. They were standing about twenty yards behind me, smiling, with bows in their hands. I started to explain that the owner had given me permission to take the photo, but they were too busy aiming to listen. Not relishing the thought of a trip to the doctor for a tetanus booster, I made a run for it.

Although I didn't get much time to study the car, which was in a New Mexico field, it appears to be a 1946 Fleetmaster Sport sedan.

Left: The Chevrolet Special Deluxe was the highest trim offering in 1940, featuring plenty of chrome, front-door armrests, and, as you can see, a pair of windshield wipers. This vehicle was found by the Old Schoolhouse in Goffs, California, a railroad town on the edge of the Mojave Desert. This tiny desert community once sat on the path of Route 66 and used to be a bustling little town and the ideal place for weary travelers to recuperate. However, the path of the Mother Road was altered in the 1930s, bypassing Goffs forever. The community should have turned into a ghost town over night, but somehow it managed to beat the odds and still exists today.

Above: After World War II, Americans were crying out for new cars. The entire auto industry had been building military vehicles for the better part of four years, and the dealerships had been empty for a long time. General Motors was eager to cash in on this unprecedented demand, wanting to get cars into showrooms as quickly as possible. There was no time to develop new models, so instead the manufacturer opted for the quicker, more cost-effective approach: reworked prewar designs. The car-starved public didn't complain; they would have bought just about anything. The cars were basically unchanged for the 1947 and 1948 model years, too, and it wasn't until 1949 that the first true postwar Chevy rolled off the production line.

A lack of bright metal around the windows indicates that this 1947 Chevrolet is an entry-level Stylemaster. Despite the idyllic setting, the photograph was taken in a Tennessee salvage yard.

Right: I have no idea what's going on with the front of this 1951 Chevrolet. Is it a belated attempt to cover the holes to prevent water from corroding the light housings, or could this be a botched attempt at frenching the headlights? Frenching is the process of doing away with the headlight rim and insetting the headlight into the fender. To do this, you first need to build up the wing so that the light then fits flush for that true 1950s kustom look.

Styleline Deluxe four-door sedans do not command a lot of money, which means this Illinois example's chances of long-term survival are slim to none.

Below: Here's another 1947 Chevy, this time a Fleetmaster Sport coupe. It was found at Wayne's Auto Salvage in Winner, South Dakota, which at the time of my visit had recently experienced a major spring cleaning. The once-legendary twenty-acre site was now just a shadow of its former self. Yard owner Wayne held a massive auction, which attracted two thousand buyers from all over the country. Around one thousand of the oldest vehicles went under the hammer during the two-day sale. Shortly afterwards, the mobile crusher disposed of another thousand less valuable vehicles. However, there are still a good number of highly desirable cars on site.

Above: It may be one of the most collectible and easily recognizable classic cars of all time, but that wasn't always the case for the 1957 Chevy. When it was new, it was shunned by a large number of would-be buyers, who opted for Fords instead. As a consequence, Chevrolet only outsold the blue oval by a couple of hundred units in 1957. It was a few years later that people realized that this was arguably the best-looking Chevy of the 1950s and possibly the best-looking Chevy ever. It never ceases to amaze me how many '57 Chevys still turn up in salvage yards and, like this one, still have an abundance of good parts to offer.

This Two-Ten four-door sedan resides in the far corner of a South Dakota yard, where it looks over the Great Plains.

Left: According to the badge on the back of this 1955 Chevy, it was originally purchased from Hoehn Chevrolet of Memphis, Tennessee, which might mean something if you are a Johnny Cash fan. Not only was the dealership just down the street from Sun Records, but it is also where Cash's brother Roy used to work. In fact, in 1955, Johnny came to visit his brother in Memphis and was introduced to mechanics (and struggling musicians) Luther Perkins and Marshall Grant, who also worked at Hoehn. The rest, as they say, is history.

This car is still in Tennessee, but today resides about ten miles away from Lynchburg, a town associated with another American legend: Jack Daniels.

Below: The windshield sunshade was a popular option in 1953 and really looks the part on this 1953 Chevy Bel Air sedan. This car is part of a large private collection of vintage vehicles belonging to Car Connection in West, Texas. The company restores classic cars, but also offers a paintwork, body repair, and parts service. Although Car Connection concentrates on 1955 to 1957 Chevys, I found a lot of different vehicles parked around the premises.

The 1953 Chevy may have looked totally different from the 1952 offering, but this was only because of a clever bit of reskinning on GM's part.

Below: This 1957 Chevy must have been involved in a serious rear-end accident for it to have snapped like this, thus destroying a rare and highly collectible automobile. As the writing on the fender says, the Chevy has a fuel-injected, 283-cubic-inch V-8 engine, which was borrowed from the Corvette. This was the first production engine to give 1 horsepower per cubic inch of displacement and not many ended up in station wagons. It seems that the original owner also forked out an extra $188 for the optional Powerglide transmission.

This vehicle is, of course, a Bel Air station wagon, one of around 27,000 built.

Above: Chevrolets built in 1958 were longer, wider, and lower than their predecessors and notable for their absence of fins. They were faster too, but only if you opted for the Turbo-Thrust V-8 with its 250-horsepower, 280-horsepower, or 315-horsepower outputs. Of course, we'll never know what engine once sat in the empty space beneath the hood of this Arkansas model.

There were three basic series for 1958: the Delray, the Biscayne, and, of course, the range-topping Bel Air (which this car is). For their hard-earned dollars, Bel Air buyers were treated to a host of luxury items not featured on the lesser cars. They also got the all-important four chevrons on the sides of the front fenders. Don't you just wish this car was on blocks in your front yard?

Left: The wide, tree-lined avenues that characterized Rio Tinto have long gone, as have most of the houses, schools, and the movie theater that were built in this Nevada copper mining town in the 1930s. When I was there, a large area had just been leveled. Bulldozers had simply pushed what appeared to be the entire town dump over the edge of a ravine. This 1957 Chevy is one of several similarly aged cars that now perch precariously on the side of the hill, and a couple have rolled all the way to the stream at the bottom of the valley.

A few bits of this vehicle's trim might be of use to someone, but that's about all.

Below: Other than a door, trunk lid, and distinctive chrome rear plate, there isn't much left of this four-door 1962 Impala SS. Gone are the electric clock, the stainless-steel window surrounds, the embossed vinyl liner headliner, and all the other goodies that buyers of these top-trim cars were treated to. This one is located near the deserted mining town of Bullfrog, Nevada, which, like the car, has definitely seen better days. When the gold ran out, many of the town's buildings were rescued and carried a mile up the road to nearby Rhyolite. But the chances of the Chevy being saved are remote.

Above: This pair of desirable station wagons was discovered by the roadside in western New Mexico. Nearest to the camera is a 1960 Chevy Kingswood, which is in amazing condition except for its flat tires. Yet somebody should close that power tailgate to ensure the interior isn't damaged by the weather. That's an equally sound 1958 Edsel Villager in the background, one of only 4,000 built. It was the midtrim station wagon in the Edsel lineup, sitting between the budget Roundup and the luxurious Bermuda.

Left: Making the most of the hot Texas sun, a 1962 Impala does a little topless sunbathing. This car was photographed several years ago in the Panhandle town of Matador. It's actually parked downtown, which, as you can see, is just as dead as the car. According to a local I met in a diner here, the town of Matador isn't a stranger to wrecked cars. Stopping only to spit wads of tobacco juice through a gaping hole where his front teeth once were, he explained that Highway 70 between Matador and Paduca is haunted and has an unexplained high number of car crashes. And what's more, since the nearest hospital is some eighty miles away, many victims do not survive.

I don't know if there's any truth in it. I'm just relaying the story.

Right: When I see a signpost for a scenic overlook, I always pull over, just on the chance there will be an abandoned car just waiting to be photographed. Needless to say, I don't find one very often. So you can imagine my disbelief when I found this 1965 Chevy Bel Air beside Highway 195 as I traveled across the Idaho-Washington border. I'm not too sure whether the car is taking in the view of Lewsiton, Idaho, or Clarkston, Washington—the towns are just a couple of miles apart.

I really hope that the car's parking brake is in better shape than its paintwork!

Below: Despite terminal corrosion and a seriously distorted rear end, this 1964 Chevy Impala SS has been saved from the crusher while hundreds of other similarly aged cars at this Pennsylvania yard have not been so lucky. Since the car clearly hasn't been spared for its bodywork, you can only assume that there's something desirable under the hood.

Back in 1964, Chevrolets were offered with a choice of seven engines and four transmissions, ranging from the uninspiring 140-horsepower six-cylinder lump to the 283-, 327-, and 409-cubic-inch V-8s.

The most powerful of the bunch had no less than 425 horses under the hood.

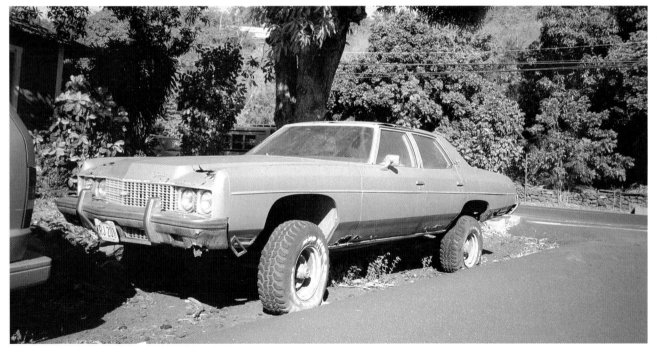

Above: Hawaii is not the best hunting ground for old cars. In fact, I've taken only one picture of an aging auto during my three trips there. Just like every island and coastal town, the abundance of salt ensures the premature demise of anything made of metal, including cars. Salt may not be put on the roads in this part of the world, but there's enough in the atmosphere to do damage. Take this 1973 Chevy, for instance, photographed on the island of Kauai. Gaping holes are appearing in the sills, doors, and even in the roof. I'm not quite sure why someone felt the need to convert this car to four-wheel drive. After all, Hawaii isn't exactly known for its adverse weather conditions.

Right: On my way to visiting the Valley of Fires lava flow, I drove past a long line of classic cars, including this 1940 Oldsmobile. They were on the outskirts of Carrizozo, in southcentral New Mexico. When this car rolled off the production line, Oldsmobile had already been building cars for four decades. This was the premier year for the company's HydraMatic gearbox, widely considered to be the best automatic transmission to date.

I have no idea who owned these cars, why they were sitting by the roadside, or what has happened to them since.

Above: LaSalle first appeared on the scene in 1927, as a way of bridging the gap between the Buick and Cadillac brands. Although sales were initially strong, the marque suffered during the Depression. While the economy made a full recovery, LaSalle did not, and General Motors pulled the plug on this short-lived make in 1940. During that time, just 205,000 had been built.

This 99-percent original Texas-based example dates to 1937, actually a strong year for LaSalle. However, a great deal of these sales were at the expense of its sibling, the Cadillac Series 60.

Left: The original Corvair's road-handling skills were so bad they inspired Ralph Nader's 1965 book *Unsafe At Any Speed*. Well, having seen the car's swimming skills, I can confirm that it is unsafe at any depth, too. This badly battered example is currently sitting in a dry riverbed, a good five hundred yards downriver from where it started out. It used to be a resident of Black Canyon Old Parts Company, in Black Canyon, Arizona, until a massive storm hit in 1993.

This arid part of Arizona is subject to flash floods, and the tiny trickle of water called Squaw Creek, which meanders past the salvage yard, became a fierce torrent of water that washed away everything in its path. Some three hundred cars were destroyed in the ensuing chaos—some washed downstream and others buried in silt, sand, and rocks. When I visited the yard in the late 1990s, a few cars, like this four-door sedan, were yet to be recovered.

I have traveled the length and breadth of Nevada in the search for old cars. Not only have I driven along every major road, but I've also covered a great deal of the dirt paths, too. One piece of advice: don't explore the back roads of the Silver State in the winter months when you need four-wheel drive because snow and mud turn these tracks into treacherous no-go areas. And another tip: watch out for landslides!

This 1953 Oldsmobile was found by the remains of a derelict mining camp in Pershing County, where it perches on top of a barrel of cyanide. So it has an excuse for looking this bad, having been stoned, shot, and poisoned.

Left, both: No, you aren't seeing things—this 1954 Oldsmobile really does have a big tree growing out of its headlight orifice. I'm actually surprised the car has been sitting around long enough for the tree to grow through it; after all, it's in excellent condition and should have been snapped up by now. Although it is now pinned to the ground, this Olds was a quick mover in its mobile days. The Rocket V-8 took the 1954 Olds to sixty miles per hour in 12.1 seconds and kept going to over one hundred miles per hour.

If you are interested in this one, you'll have to visit Eastern Nebraska Auto Sales in Elmwood. Be sure to take a saw with you.

Below: I'm mystified as to why someone cut a hole in the passenger door of this 1957 Oldsmobile or why the hood is so badly deformed. It's one of thirteen thousand cars at French Lake Auto Parts in Minnesota. Despite having been dissected, the Olds is still in pretty good shape. It appears to be a Golden Rocket 88 four-door hardtop Fiesta station wagon and since only 5,767 were built, it deserves to be saved.

The 1957 model was promoted as the most altered Oldsmobile in twenty years. Its design changes included being longer, lower, and a little bit wider than the previous year's model. It was also the first time in seven years that station wagons appeared in the Oldsmobile lineup.

Compared with the shack in the background, this 1954 Oldsmobile 88 is in incredibly good condition. (I have a sneaky suspicion you would only need to sneeze in the vicinity of the building for it to completely collapse.) Just a few hundred yards from the car is the Goldfield (Nevada) Hotel, widely considered the most impressive hotel west of the Mississippi when it was built. The four-story building, which is in remarkably good condition despite not hosting guests since the 1940s, has an automotive claim to fame: it's where the blind DJ ran his pirate radio station in the classic car-chase film *Vanishing Point*.

Right: A badly vandalized 1972 Oldsmobile Delta Holiday 88 four-door hardtop is parked close to one of Nevada's numerous legal brothels. I wonder how the vehicle ended up in this horrible mess. Do you think maybe one of the ladies yanked the wires and put her stiletto heels through the windshield when the owner failed to pay for services rendered?

Check out all that tidy sheet metal, which is typical of cars from arid desert climates. Rust-belt dwellers can only dream of finding a nonrestored car from this era in this condition.

Below: It's not often that you find one 1967 Oldsmobile Delmont 88 convertible in this condition, much less a pair of identical examples. Ragtop Delmonts came with a 425-cubic-inch V-8 as standard, although both of these models in a Minnesota yard have lost theirs. The one closest to the camera has a badly deteriorated interior, too, but the other has retained its roof and fared considerably better.

I wonder how many of the other 3,525 Delmont convertibles from 1967 have survived.

Nineteen thirty-four Pontiacs are hard to find these days. After all, total production was fewer than 80,000 that year, and only a tiny percentage have survived. Yet I find it hard to believe that Windy Hill Auto Parts in Minnesota has bothered to save this sorry example, as it doesn't seem to have a lot going for it. I'm struggling to see what, if anything, can still be salvaged from the pitiful wreck.

The Pontiac Buggy Company, of Pontiac, Michigan, first built horse-drawn carriages in 1893, and it wasn't until 1926 that its first cars appeared.

This Pontiac, on the other hand, has a lot more going for it. The engine may have disappeared, but take a look at all those rust-free body panels. It even has most of its glass, preserving the interior. That silver streak running down the trunk lid indicates this is a Pontiac, and the lack of chrome strips running along the front and rear fenders make me believe we are looking at a 1948 Streamliner four-door sedan. It was originally offered with a choice of six- or eight-cylinder engines, but the vast majority of buyers opted for the larger of the two.

It's amazing what you can find on a stroll through the Tennessee countryside. Someone has scribbled "$200" on the smashed windshield of this car, which seems like a fair price to pay for a 1950 Pontiac. But on reflection, what are you actually getting for your money? The vehicle has no driveline, a badly damaged interior, very little glass, and if you are extra quiet you can probably hear it rusting.

Pontiacs built in 1950 were virtually identical to the previous year's models; the horizontal center grille bar that wraps around the bodywork is one of the few differences.

Above: Pick up your atlas and look up Warm Springs, Nevada. You'll find it at the junction where Highway 375 meets Highway 6. Looks like a reasonably sized town, doesn't it? Perhaps large enough for a couple of diners, some gas stations, and a motel? That's what I thought when I planned to fill up with gas there on a drive from Battle Mountain to Las Vegas. However, not only does Warm Springs not have a gas station, but it also doesn't have a single person living there. All you'll find is an abandoned restaurant, a bunch of old mining shacks, and what I'm guessing was once a 1951 Pontiac coupe.

I eventually ran out of gas about ten miles from the town of Rachel, but a passing motorist was kind enough to sell me a gallon—for twenty dollars!

Right: "We have placed more emphasis on the sculpturing of sheet metal, less on brightwork," Pontiac General Manager Semon E. Knudsen said about the 1959 cars. The results were one of the more recognizable tailfins to appear that year and the birth of Pontiac's soon-to-be trademark split grille. Knudsen was also responsible for widening the car at the last minute, creating the first "widetrack" Pontiac. It not only looked great, but also rode and cornered better than just about anything else built in America that year. The enticing package was completed with the Tempest V-8 engine, powering the car to sixty miles per hour in less than ten seconds.

This Texas example is a prestigious Bonneville Vista four-door hardtop, one of less than 40,000 made.

Below: This 1957 Pontiac Star Chief Custom Safari may be ultra rare, but unfortunately it is as rotten as a withering pear. Although it is located in the center of the Lone Star State, the massive amounts of rust indicate it isn't Texas born and bred. I'm assuming the tailgate was in slightly better condition than the rest of the bodywork because it has been cut off.

The Safari was Pontiac's answer to the Chevy Nomad, although it didn't sell nearly as well. In fact, just 1,292 of these found buyers, compared with more than 6,000 of the Chevrolets. This was the last of the model's three-year production run.

Widetrack Pontiacs were just as wide in 1960 as their 1959 predecessors, as demonstrated by this two-door hardtop sport coupe. That trunk lid was very nearly large enough to land a light aircraft on. The Bonneville was Pontiac's top-trim offering at the time, and the $3,257 price tag was justified with sweeteners like padded dashboards with walnut inserts, courtesy lamps, and a four-barrel V-8. The car looks as though it just needs a new battery before it can be driven out of this yard, but if it were that simple, it probably wouldn't have ended up here in the first place.

   If you think you've got a garage wide enough to accommodate it, you'll want to get in touch with Vintage Auto Salvage in Bradford, Arkansas. Be warned, though; the picture was taken in 2001, so someone may have beaten you to it.

In 1961, GM introduced three new smaller cars, including the Pontiac Tempest. The newcomer featured a new four-cylinder powerplant, created by cutting a V-8 in half. It had a top speed of 102 miles per hour and could manage the quarter mile in twenty seconds. The split grille launched on the 1959 offerings had proven to be a massive hit, but Pontiac's designers hadn't expected their handiwork to be so popular. They deleted it from the 1960 cars. It was back by popular demand in 1961 and became a trademark Pontiac feature.

Although $750 isn't an unreasonable price to ask for a one-owner 1961 Tempest, I'm not sure how truthful the seller is being with the "will run" claim. You see, there isn't actually anything under the hood. So unless your journey home is downhill all the way, it might take a while to get back. That's used car salesmen for you.

CHAPTER 4

❖

THE
INDEPENDENTS

*"The reason American cars don't sell anymore is that they
have forgotten how to design the American Dream. What
does it matter if you buy a car today or six months from now,
because cars are not beautiful."*
— Karl Lagerfeld, fashion designer, 1992

The "sharknose" Graham is one of the most distinctive cars ever built. Unfortunately,
this Graham's magnificent hood and grille have long since been liberated and their
absence has totally altered the car's appearance. By the time this 1939 example was
built, the Graham-Paige Motors Corporation was struggling. The sharknose had
nose-dived, and the company was running out of options. Although the car plant was
closed in 1940, that wasn't the end of the story. The corporation later became an
investment company and went on to own New York's Madison Square Garden.
Judging by the date on its door, this Graham arrived at Minnesota's French Lake
Auto Parts in July 2000 and was photographed five years later.

Below: The grain silo in the background gives this location away as Danville, Kansas. The car, a 1958 Rambler Rebel Custom Cross Country, was photographed at the Bob Lint Motor Shop in the late 1990s. At the time, this small yard had been at its present location for well over three decades and had built up an amazing collection of old cars.

A little more than 3,000 of these V-8-powered station wagons found buyers, and today they seem to have all but disappeared. Nineteen fifty-eight was a recession year, but AMC sales were strong. In fact, Rambler finished the year in seventh position. Two years later, it had climbed to an incredible fourth place, behind Chevrolet, Ford, and Plymouth.

Above: American Motors Corporation (AMC) formed in 1954 after the merger of a pair of independents: Nash-Kelvinator and Hudson. The two makes were allowed to continue until 1958, at which point both names were dropped and the company concentrated on a revised series of vehicles. At the heart of this new lineup was the Rambler American, basically a rehashed 1955 Nash Rambler. It may have been old, but it was cheap—exactly what was needed in a recession.

This is a 1958 model, a two-door Rambler American Super to be exact. It is easy to differentiate from the cheaper Deluxe by the metal window surrounds and the beltline trim. The car was photographed in a central Kansas town in 1997.

Left: The 1959 Rambler Six Deluxe four-door sedan cost $2,098 and was the cheapest offering in the AMC model lineup that year. These low-cost cars were starved of interior luxuries, and the external differences ensured that other motorists knew you couldn't afford the dearer Super version. The Deluxe not only lacked side trim, but also had only dual headlamps as an option.

This vehicle was photographed at Lyman Auto Wreckers in McGill, Nevada, on a bitterly cold November morning in 2002. It is one of several hundred similarly aged vehicles sprawled over the forty-acre site at the edge of the Humboldt National Forest.

Right: It may have been photographed in Georgia, but you certainly couldn't describe this Gremlin as a peach. When was the last time you saw an AMC Gremlin driving past? Not only are they scarcely seen on the streets these days, but there aren't too many left in salvage yards either. Introduced in 1970 (on April Fool's Day), the Gremlin was a rushed attempt at combating the growing number of foreign cars that were flying out of dealers' showrooms. Essentially half a Hornet, it was hailed as America's first home-built subcompact. It was supposed to go head-to-head with the Volkswagen Bug, but did anyone actually brief the car's designers on this?

The car managed no more than seventeen miles per gallon, far from what fuel-conscious buyers were after. As the number of imports continued to grow, so did the Gremlin's engine. Two years after its launch, it was offered with a 304-cubic-inch V-8.

Above: AMC made a few mistakes over the years, but here's one the marque definitely got right. The Javelin was introduced in September 1967, making it the last and, in many people's eyes, the best pony car. That was certainly a feat, considering that AMC was hardly synonymous with performance. Behind the wheel, the car felt as good as it looked. With its 343-cubic-inch V-8, this SST sport coupe could reach sixty miles per hour in just over eight seconds, with a quarter mile passing by in 15.4 seconds. The SST had all the usual goodies, with the addition of front bucket seats, a sports steering wheel, and a hood scoop.

This Javelin was photographed in a Casa Grande, Arizona, salvage yard.

Left: With some shoes on its feet, this lonely AMC Pacer wouldn't look out of place on the highway—at least no more than when it was originally on the road. Considering this Pacer was found in a South Dakota salvage yard, it is in amazing condition—from the flawless bodywork to the pristine interior. The car even retains all the windows that helped earn it the "glass egg" nickname. The Pacer was christened "the first wide small car" and was supposed to fight off fuel-efficient compact imports from Japan and Europe. However, the car's six-cylinder engine had other ideas, returning just eighteen miles per gallon and failing to top one hundred miles per hour.

I know this isn't everyone's idea of a classic car, but the AMC Pacer is one of the world's most instantly identifiable cars. In my eyes, it has rightfully earned a place in history and on the pages of this book. I confess I have a bit of a soft spot for Pacers, but judging by how few survive, I'm probably the only one.

Above: Yes, somebody really has taken the time and effort to transform an AMC Eagle woody into a tractor. Well, I don't think the John Deere bosses are going to have too many sleepless nights over it. The Concord-based 4x4 Eagle was introduced in 1980 and it was a good attempt at combining truck-like handling with the comfort and luxury of a sedan. But the market for such a vehicle was limited, and Eagles never flew out of the showrooms. The car stayed in production for most of the decade, though. The last ones rolled off the line in 1988. The Eagle was arguably a decade ahead of its time; after all, how different is this from today's Subaru sports-utility sedans?

Right: Crosley production actually started in 1939, but sales really took off with the introduction of the make's popular station wagon in 1947. With its extra internal space and simulated wood paneling (which you can't see on this example because of rust), it was an instant success. It was soon the best seller in the range. And just like the sedan, its 44-cubic-inch four-cylinder engine returned a frugal forty to fifty miles per gallon.

The dome on the front of this car dates it to 1947 or 1948, which makes it one of fewer than 25,000 built. It was photographed behind an unused shop on the Utah-Nevada border.

Below: Powel Crosley Jr. had a dream: he wanted to give the American public a basic, low-cost car, which he did in the 1940s. His timing was impeccable, as post–World War II Americans were desperate for automobiles and happy to drive just about anything. At $905, a 1946 Crosley sedan was certainly cheap, but buyers didn't get a whole lot for their bucks. They had to dig deeper if they wanted such luxuries as a heater, radio, or even turn signals.

This Crosley, photographed behind a shop in Grand Island, Nebraska, appears to be one of the final facelift cars and dates to 1951 or 1952. It is an extremely rare automobile, as only 1,300 sedans were built over this two-year period.

Above: The Essex was apparently named after the English county with the same name because owner Hudson supposedly wanted a car with snob appeal. But how times have changed. Today, the county of Essex is synonymous with peroxide-blonde teenage mothers whose boyfriends drive clapped out Ford Escorts with expensive sound systems. The make was introduced in 1919 and survived for thirteen years. Although the Essex brand effectively died in 1932, the cars were built under the Terraplane banner until 1938. If I'm not mistaken, this two-door coupe dates to around 1929. It is parked next to a couple of other old cars, one of which has the words "No It's Not" painted on the window. This indicates that its owners are fed up with people asking whether the cars are for sale. With that in mind, I'm not going to reveal which Utah town I photographed these in.

Right: By the time this 1949 (or possibly 1950) Frazer was built, sales were tumbling fast, and the writing was on the wall for the marque. Frazer shared its basic body style with Kaiser, but it cost a few hundred dollars more than its sibling—enough to ensure that it was the worst seller of the pair. Total production in 1949 and 1950 was just 25,000 units, compared with almost 100,000 Kaisers. Although Kaiser continued to exist until the mid-1950s, the plug was pulled on Frazer in 1951.

This four-door Manhattan was photographed outside a closed Oklahoma salvage yard.

Below: The Kaiser-Frazer Corporation was the last independent challenger to "the Big Three" automakers, and in the beginning it was a serious contender. It beat Ford, Chrysler, and GM in the race to build a true postwar car and the modern straight-sided cars sold well. But the big boys were hot on its heels, and sales soon began to dwindle.

This Frazer Standard, photographed in a Las Vegas yard that no longer exists, appears to be an original 1947 model. Of course, none of the thirty-five changes introduced for the 1948 model year are particularly obvious, so I could be a year off.

The Graham brothers started out building trucks and sold out to Dodge Brothers in 1926. But two years later, they were back with their new Graham-Paige automobile (the Paige part of the name was dropped in 1930). The company suffered during the Depression, but by the time this 1936 Cavalier was built, sales were on the up again—albeit temporarily.

Not only is this Arizona example relatively rust free and structurally sound, but the interior is also packed with spare parts. It was photographed at Wiseman's Auto Salvage. But where is it today?

A tired Henry J leans against a tree for support in central Texas. Kaiser-Frazer was under the impression that its new "people's car" would be the next Model T, but the automaker was way off. In 1951, the Henry J's debut year, some 82,000 found buyers, but the novelty quickly wore off. Sales fell steadily from this point onward; only 1,119 found buyers in 1954, its final year. Henry J buyers were offered a choice of four- or six-cylinder engines, achieving top speeds of seventy-five miles per hour and eighty-five miles per hour, respectively. These engines reached sixty miles per hour within twenty-five and fifteen seconds, respectively. However, in the 1960s, many were used as drag racers because the vehicles were so light. In order to keep prices low, these cars lacked anything in the way of creature comforts. Not only did the spartan Henry J lack sun visors and a glove-compartment lid, but it also didn't even get an opening trunk. The car was also marketed as an Allstate and sold through Sears Roebuck department stores.

Below: This 1942 Hudson is coincidentally a great advertisement for the nearby antiques shop in Offerle, Kansas. It's a Commodore four-door sedan, one of just 40,661 Hudsons built prior to February 5, when production halted due to World War II. The faded poster in the window says $900 is enough to buy this heavyweight Hudson, but without a grille and trim, this car must be lighter than its original 3,400 pounds. New for 1942 were flared doors to hide running boards and a foot control for the radio. Positioned between the clutch and the brake pedals, the foot control could be used to change channels and even to mute the volume.

Above: The first true postwar Hudsons arrived in 1948 and were well worth the wait. Of course, you wouldn't think so if this was the only example you had ever seen. The "step-down" Hudsons were sleek, low-slung, aerodynamic, and incredibly stylish. They not only looked great, but they also had road-holding manners to match, thanks to an exceptionally low center of gravity.

As great as the design was, these cars did outstay their welcome. Sales peaked at 159,100 in 1949 and then steadily declined. By 1952, the figure had more than halved. Hudson badly needed a replacement, but it was cash starved, having just sunk a fortune into the 1953 Jet.

This severely corroded wreck, which looks like it must have been involved in a serious collision before being dumped on its roof in a river, was found at Ace Auto Salvage in Illinois.

Left: Hudson's postwar offerings were similar to its prewar cars; in fact, they were virtually identical. The key distinguishing features of this 1947 Super two-door sedan are its grille and front bumper, although they are only slightly different from the 1946 versions. Most Hudsons from this era were specified with fender-mounted lamps, but the original owner of this one clearly didn't think they were worth the extra sixteen dollars. However, he did decide to part with three hard-earned bucks for a passenger sun visor because, contrary to the impression given by this photograph, Texas actually does get a lot of sun.

This car was one of several destitute classics I photographed in San Diego, Texas.

Below: An elderly man, who was tinkering with the machinery you see in the background, told me this Commodore four-door sedan would one day be restored, but I have my doubts. From this angle, it is impossible to determine whether this is a 1948 or 1949 car. In fact, the only differences between the two years were inside and consisted of not much more than different carpeting.

Notice how the car is dwarfed by the rotting log in the background. The log is a giant redwood and presumably came from the nearby California redwood forests.

Above: By 1955, Hudson had joined forces with Nash-Kelvinator to form AMC, which explains why the step-down replacement was basically a badge-engineered Nash—or Hash. One of the most desirable models that year was this Hornet Custom Hollywood hardtop, which has been abandoned at the end of a dirt road not too far away from a Colorado junkyard. These cars were pricey at $2,880 and didn't sell well. Only a little more than 3,000 found customers, who bought an almost even mix of six-cylinder and V-8 engines.

This model has the optional continental wheel mount, extending the rear bumper by ten inches.

Left: When did you last see this many step-downs in one place? They are part of a private collection of Hudsons I found on the outskirts of Challis, Idaho, in 2004. I spent many hours with my head in reference books trying to identify the car on the left and finally decided it must be 1951 Hornet. The confusion arose because it has been fitted with a Commodore 6 fender, complete with identification badge. This modification was possible because the Hornet was basically identical to the Commodore, only with a high-performance engine and some different trim.

In the middle is a four-door 1952 Pacemaker, which was the cheapest car in the model lineup that year. And on the right, priced roughly $150 more that same year, is a slightly plusher Wasp.

In addition to the Hornet, Hudson's other 1955 offering was the Rambler, which, like the Hornet, was nothing more than a thinly disguised Nash. It was even trimmed and priced the same as the equivalent Nash models, the only differences being its grille, badges, and hubcaps. Not content with buying the most expensive car in the Rambler lineup, the original owner of this Custom Cross Country station wagon went a bit crazy with the options list, specifying both air conditioning ($345) and the Weather Eye heater and defroster ($77).

The vehicle may be a little frayed around the edges, but it's basically sound, almost complete, and extremely restorable. The Pininfarina-styled car can be found at Watts Repair Salvage & Auto in Nebraska, along with thousands of other pre-1975 classics.

Windy Hill Auto Parts in Minnesota is one of very few salvage yards that can claim to be breaking a 1927 Hupmobile. In 1909, the Hupp Motor Company started to build its workingman's car: the Hupmobile. Sales were slow to begin with but had grown to more than 38,000 units per year by 1923. Three years later, the automaker was offering a comprehensive range of cars with four-, six-, and eight-cylinder engines.

Like most car makers, Hupp suffered during the Depression years and never made a full recovery. It did put up a brave fight, acquiring the tooling for the defunct Cord in the late 1930s, but the project was doomed. In its death throes, the company set up a deal with Graham-Paige (which wasn't doing well financially itself), whereby the latter would manufacture the Cord-based Skylark for Hupp and a similar car for itself. But Hupp's days were over and it was forced to leave the car industry for good in 1940. During its thirty years, it built half a million cars, including Detroit's first police car.

Like the body of a decaying animal stripped of its flesh by hungry vultures, this Jeep has absolutely no parts left, thanks to scavengers. It may be one of the most dilapidated, shot up, battered, abused wrecks I've ever photographed, but it is still instantly identifiable as a Commando. This model, which was produced between 1967 and 1971, was a modern version of the original Jeepster. Distinctive styling features included a wider-than-usual hood, which overlapped the front fenders. I found it in the desert near the town of Beatty, Nevada, while testing the off-road ability of a brand new Cadillac Sedan DeVille rental car.

Left: By 1953, when this four-door Deluxe rolled off the line, Kaiser was beginning to struggle. Model-year production had fallen to about 31,000, and things were about to get a whole lot worse. In 1954, production was down to less than 6,000 units, and a year later Kaiser became just another name in the history books. Cars built in 1953 were very similar to the previous year's models because of a lack of development funds. The introduction of chrome tailfins was one design change on this car, certainly nothing that cost a fortune to add.

This example wants rescuing from South Side Salvage in Salida, Colorado, where at 3,200 pounds it dwarfs the neighboring MG Midget.

Below: After World War II, shipbuilder Henry J. Kaiser teamed up with Joseph Frazer and started building cars with some success. In fact, this 1951 example is one of 145,000 Kaisers built that year. The Kaiser marque was something of a pioneer. It is credited as being one of the first automakers to offer seat belts and pop-out windshields. It also developed the Vagabond, a unique hatchback sedan.

This is a Deluxe Club coupe and a resident of a Mountain Home, Idaho, salvage yard. Wouldn't you just love to spend a few hours exploring this place?

Above: The original Lafayette Motors Company, which was the brainchild of Charles Nash, built cars between 1921 and 1924. It was run as a separate entity to Nash, and its products were supposedly better quality than rival Cadillac. However, by 1924 just 2,267 Lafayette vehicles had attracted buyers, which wasn't a large enough volume to warrant the marque's existence. In 1934, the name was resurrected, but this time as a lower-priced Nash.

This 1937 four-door sedan, discovered at Snyder Brothers Garage & Auto Wrecking in Texas, is in fantastic condition. It's almost complete too, although I'm not sure that those headlights or bolt-on turn lamps are original.

Right: This two-tone Metropolitan has been dragged out of the undergrowth a few years too late, as the damage has already been done. Trees are notoriously bad for cars, and the humidity in southern Tennessee has only aggravated the problem. As a result, the car has more holes than a bald porcupine.

Metropolitans still have a strong following today and paying $400 would be a good deal for a complete one. However, the rust on this late model is terminal, and the car seems barely able to support its own weight. Although this car still has its original Austin-built engine under the hood, it's unlikely to ever harness those fifty-two horses again!

Below: America's first subcompact wasn't that American at all. In fact, you could argue it was the first true global car. Although it was the brainchild of Nash-Kelvinator's George Mason, it was partly penned in Italy by Pininfarina and built in England. It even had Austin running gear and was marketed in the United Kingdom with an Austin badge on its grille. The Metropolitan's real success was stateside, though, where it was sold as both a Nash and Hudson before becoming a marque of its own in 1957. Between 1945 and 1960, some 95,000 were produced.

This picture was taken at the entrance to Lyman Auto Wreckers, where a light dusting of snow had fallen on Nevada's Schell Creek Range.

Above: L&L Classic Auto in Wendell, Idaho, has a whole field of very restorable cars like this one, many of which are yet to be parted out. The exterior might look a bit crusty, but it's structurally sound, making it not too expensive to put this car back on the road. The vehicle is a 1942 Nash Ambassador four-door sedan, which is something of a rarity. America was gearing up to go to war in 1942 and cut car production short that year. Fewer than 5,500 Nashes were built in 1942. The cars were actually very similar to the previous model year's, with a new grille and fender-mounted turn signals being the most significant changes.

Right: The "bathtub" Nash, launched in 1949 as the Airflyte series, was considered America's first aerodynamic car. It was years ahead of the competition in a number of respects. Unfortunately, that didn't do the company much good in the long run, as the marque vanished in 1958. The entry-level Nash 600 was renamed the Statesman for 1950. This vehicle appears to be one of the renamed classics, the four-door Super, which was the basic trim offering and the best seller. It is pictured at the entrance to a Nebraska salvage yard, where it so far has managed to avoid being picked over by parts hunters.

Below: Would you be allowed to park this car on the street where you live without fear it would be towed away? I guess that is one of the benefits of living in what is virtually a ghost town. The 1948 Nash, which looks as though it has been dropped on its roof, was parked outside a house in Goldfield, Nevada. However, dealing with old junked cars isn't high on the town's agenda, as it has a more pressing waste-management problem to worry about. There are plans afoot to turn nearby Yucca Mountain into the United States' first licensed national repository for high-level radioactive waste and spent nuclear fuel. And there's a good chance that waste will all be rolling though town on its way to the dump.

Below: New for the 1951 Nash Airflyte models were extended and raised rear fenders with incorporated taillights. The revised design ruined the "beetleback" appearance, which wasn't a bad thing in some people's eyes. Among the Airflyte's many innovative design features was the Uniscope, a teardrop-shaped device that was attached to the steering column and housed all the instruments. The Uniscope housing is just visible inside this full-size Ambassador Super four-door sedan.

This 1951 Ambassador, photographed in Nebraska, had 115 horses under its hood, courtesy of the six-cylinder engine. They galloped to a top speed of ninety-five miles per hour, reaching sixty miles per hour in eighteen seconds.

Above: A distinct lack of side chrome made for a refreshing styling change in 1955, especially for a luxury car like this Nash Ambassador Super. The uncluttered styling, with headlights enclosed in a new oval concave grille and wraparound windshield, was partly the handiwork of Pininfarina (although the Italian stylist's contribution is actually believed to have been minimal).

What the car lacked in brightwork, it more than made up for with interior fitments. The top-line Nash came with reclining seats and, of course, the respected Weather-Eye ventilation system. Also new for 1955 models was a 320-cubic-inch V-8 Clipper engine, courtesy of Packard. With this under the hood, the Ambassador was good for over one hundred miles per hour, although acceleration hardly induced whiplash. Whether this Nebraska car was fitted with a six- or an eight-cylinder is pretty much irrelevant, as there's nothing under its hood today.

The final Nash Ambassador rolled off the Kenosha, Wisconsin, production line in the summer of 1957, but the Ambassador name continued to exist until 1974.

Left: Here's another 1951 bathtub Nash, relatively unmolested by parts scavengers. It stands a good chance of being saved from this Texas salvage yard. In fact, it is just several gallons of paint and a new headlight away from looking like a semirespectable car again.

Although the Airflyte sold better than any other big Nash in history, it was falling out of public favor by 1951. In later years, the car-buying public turned its back on big Nash cars altogether, resulting in the marque's demise in 1957.

Packard is one of America's oldest car makers, tracing its history to the end of the nineteenth century. The company rapidly gained a reputation for building quality automobiles, concentrating on superior build quality rather than up-to-the-minute styling changes. While this proved to be a sensible philosophy during the pre-World War II years, it wasn't what postwar Americans wanted. And by the time Packard caught on to this, the company didn't have the finances to develop the supply of new designs the car-buying public craved.

As a result, the 1950s were a turbulent time for Packard, and the decision to purchase Studebaker didn't help its cause. Studebaker had problems of its own. Both 1957 and 1958 Packards were no more than badge-engineered Studebakers and didn't sell well. It was a sad end to another once-proud name.

This 1940 Packard, which still has a few bits and pieces to offer, was photographed in 2005 at French Lake Auto Parts in Minnesota.

Check out this rare Packard Clipper Deluxe Eight. It's not often that you find one in this sorry state, especially not with the hood ornament still in place. It's difficult to say whether this four-door sedan hails from 1942, 1946, or 1947, as these vehicles were virtually identical. The car is part of a private collection of about thirty vehicles that I stumbled upon in a central Texas town. The owner, who allowed me to explore the site unaccompanied, requested that I don't reveal its whereabouts. Unfortunately, I never got the chance to ask him why several of the other cars (including the 1955 Studebaker Commander next to the Packard) have been completely covered in what appears to be turquoise paint.

This once-fine 1948 Packard has a degrading existence, now that it has been abandoned in a field of cows. I discovered this vandalized wreck a few years back, while I was trying to retrace Route 66 through New Mexico. It was sitting by the roadside, on the other side of a barbed-wire fence, somewhere south of Santa Fe.

As for the exact identity of this four-door sedan, I'm not sure. I can say with confidence that it isn't a Custom Eight, so either it's a Standard Eight or Super Eight. Either way, the car has been parked here for too many years to be of use to anyone now.

The Peerless Motor Company of Cleveland, Ohio, started building cars at the turn of the twentieth century. It produced high-quality, luxury automobiles, and its sales were strong. But then, in the late 1920s, the Great Depression hit, and luxury cars were the last thing the market needed. Peerless was quick to feel the pinch and, like so many other independent companies, it was forced to close its doors. The last car rolled off the line in 1931.

This four-door sedan, which probably dates to around 1930, was found in an Idaho yard. It's clearly not in good shape and stands very little chance of being rescued.

Below: This 1928 Studebaker Dictator looks like it has been used in a suicide bomb attack, although I'm not sure that this Arizona junkyard would be a probable target. The truth is that someone has cut the rear end off, including the roof support, which has caused the aging car to totally collapse. When this vehicle was built, Studebaker was already more than seventy-five years old, having started building horse-drawn carts in 1852. At one point, the South Bend, Indiana, manufacturer was the world's largest producer of horse-drawn vehicles.

Above: A Texas hedgerow is home to this 1937 Studebaker Dictator four-door sedan. Other than losing its sight in one eye, the car is in amazingly good shape and has even managed to hold onto its optional fender-mounted parking lamps and side-mounted spare wheel. The 1937 Dictator featured a new front end, with a one-piece hood that was raised from the front.

It's a resident of Snyder Brothers Garage & Auto Wrecking—well worth a visit if you ever find yourself in central Texas.

Left: I was a little disappointed by my visit to Arizona's Petrified Forest National Park, as there wasn't a whole lot of petrified wood to see. Of course, there certainly was no shortage of it in the numerous gift shops I passed for the next thirty miles or so. Perhaps that's why the rangers insisted on searching my truck before I was allowed to leave the park. But the journey wasn't a complete waste. I did come across this petrified Studebaker just a short distance from the park. I think it was built in 1932, give or take a year or two.

Despite having lost its huge hood and unique grille, there's no mistaking this 1939 Studebaker Commander four-door sedan. It's another relic from Goldfield, a former mining camp and semi–ghost town about 150 miles north of Las Vegas, Nevada.

Over the years, the car has been stripped of all salvageable parts and what's left has been severely vandalized. I'm sure such behavior wouldn't have been tolerated one hundred years earlier when Virgil Earp, brother of Wyatt Earp, was a lawman in this town. I'm not sure if anyone actually owns this and the other cars scattered around the edge of town.

This Studebaker Commander rolled off the line in 1952, the same year the company celebrated its one hundredth anniversary. But storm clouds were brewing at Studebaker. The milestone year wasn't one big champagne-swilling party. With an aging factory and a lack of investment, financial strife soon hit. Just two years later, the company was purchased by Packard.

The big model in 1952 was this vehicle: the Starliner pillarless hardtop. This long-awaited body style was an instant hit. The Starliner accounted for 15 percent of Studebaker sales in its first year. The car was photographed in Whitney, Texas.

Right: In 1959, Americans were crying out for economy cars, so the Lark landed at just the right time. In fact, you can argue this car single-handedly prolonged the existence of its ailing carmaker. The Lark's introductory year was a great one for Studebaker, as sales were higher than they had been since the early 1950s. But by 1960, the Big Three also offered compacts, and all of a sudden the Lark was not flying near as high as it had been. The Lark name survived until 1964, but its early success was never replicated.

This is an original Lark VI four-door sedan, but from this angle it's impossible to determine whether it is a 1959 or a 1960 car. Either way, this is not a particularly desirable automobile and probably doesn't warrant been dragged from the Michigan undergrowth.

Above: The 1962 Studebaker Gran Turismo Hawk two-door hardtop came equipped with a 289-cubic-inch V-8 engine, although this badly damaged example had its heart ripped out. The car presumably came to Ace Auto Salvage in Illinois after being involved in a accident that caused serious front-end damage. This car may not be a viable restoration project, but it would certainly make a great parts donor for somebody restoring an early 1960s Gran Turismo.

Left: Back in 1956, this President Classic four-door sedan was a real head turner, and priced at $2,489, it was second only in cost to the Golden Hawk. Although the company's financial troubles prevented a total redesign, Studebakers built in 1956 did receive a revamped interior that included a unique cyclops-eye speedometer, which rotated to show the vehicle's speed. It changed from green to orange and to red as the car's speed increased.

Although the exterior on this model is pretty sound, the same cannot be said for the interior. Unfortunately, somebody left the windows open, and what little moisture this part of Arizona receives has played havoc with the upholstery. The seats, headliner, and trim are totally rotten, and the dashboard is beginning to rust. Only 8,507 President Classic models were built in 1956, and La Palma Auto and Truck Salvage in Arizona is the only salvage yard where I have seen one.

This sorry-looking Willys-Knight four-door sedan sits within the boundaries of a small salvage yard on Highway 93 between Kingman, Arizona, and the Hoover Dam. I'm told it's a 1926 Great Six, and who am I to argue? The company traces its origins back to 1908 when John North Willys bought the Overland Automotive Division of Standard Wheel Company, renaming it Willys-Overland Motor Company in 1912. A year later, the company acquired a license to build Knight engines, which it marketed as the Willys-Knight. Over the next few years, Willys-Overland became America's second-largest car manufacturer, second only to Ford. Eventually, its success would change.

Thank you, Floyd Nolan, owner of French Lake Auto Parts, for scribbling "31-32 Willys" on the side of this car, as it certainly saved me some time paging though reference books. Although the company was a successful car builder, it really became known for a very different product: the jeep. Just prior to World War II, Willys-Overland began building a lightweight truck, based on an American Bantam design, for the U.S. Army.

The Willys Jeep was an instant success, and after the war, the vehicle manufacturer temporarily turned its back on all car production, solely producing civilian jeeps. Today the company still survives in the form of Jeep, a subsidiary of DaimlerChrysler.

This 1941 Willys Americar sits by the roadside in a desolate a west Texas town, where it has been used for target practice. The patriotically named Americar, the only car in the Willys lineup that year, featured a shark-nose hood and flush headlamps.. With these features, it didn't look too different from Fords of the same era. In the 1960s, these lightweight, short-wheelbase cars became desirable when drivers discovered they were perfect for drag racing. It's certainly rare to find an abandoned one these days.

Kaiser overtook Willys-Overland in 1953, and two years later it decided to pull the plug on all Willys passenger cars. Before it did, though, there was just enough time to give the Aero lineup a facelift and a new name for the final model year. This rare 1955 four-door Custom, one of just 2,882 four-door sedans built, was one of the last Willys cars built in America. When Kaiser-Willys pulled out of the American passenger car market, the specifications for this car were shipped to Brazil, where it was made for several years.

This photograph was taken at an Oregon car dealer, AA Auto Sales. The car is one of a lot of classics that had been rescued from woodland. It is a sound car, both inside and out, and hopefully has been saved.

CHAPTER 5

SPECIAL VEHICLES

"No illusion is more crucial than the illusion that great success and huge money buy you immunity from the common ills of mankind, such as cars that won't start."
— Larry McMurtry, author of Lonesome Dove

By the time this truck was built, Diamond T commercial vehicles had been around for more than forty years. In fact, the famous diamond emblem was designed a few decades earlier than that—to identify the family shoe-making business. After forty-seven years of independence, the company was purchased by rival White, which already owned truck manufacturer REO. Although Diamond T's production facility was promptly closed, it kept its identity until 1966, when it merged with REO to form Diamond REO.

This picture was taken in 1996 near Pratt, Kansas.

Below: Old school buses never die—they just get used as spare sheds. I don't think I've been to a junkyard that doesn't have at least a handful of yellow buses scattered around, packed to the rafters with spare parts. French Lake Auto Parts in Minnesota has a whole row of them—each identified by its own letter. Take a close look at Bus C, which had an unusual previous owner. I'm assuming Hart's Nudist Camp only operates in the summer months because you certainly wouldn't want to be running around in your birthday suit during the Minnesota winter.

Above: The Rocky Mountain foothills are not the backdrop you expect to see behind a Checker cab. This cab looks like a fish out of water away from the hustle and bustle of New York City. The Checker, perhaps the most instantly recognizable car ever built, is an American icon, up there with Harley-Davidson and Peterbilt. Its popularity ensures that few ever appear in salvage yards.

It's hard to put an exact age on this vehicle, although those five mile per hour safety bumpers were introduced in 1974. The cab was in a salvage yard in Salida, Colorado, and is in excellent condition. Most of the panels are clean, and there aren't even any dents in those huge bumpers.

Left: According to a guy I met at Wiseman's Auto Salvage, who was removing some interior trim from this car, it is a 1951 Crown Imperial limousine. If he's right, it is one of the most rare vehicles featured in this book. Only 338 examples were built during the two-year period between 1951 and 1952. At $6,740, these luxurious limos were at least $3,000 more expensive than the regular Imperial four-door sedan. But by buying the limo, you got an extra fourteen inches of automobile, more than enough room for eight passengers.

Right: Wouldn't this eight-passenger 1961 Oldsmobile make a fantastic alternative to the stretched Town Cars, Hummers, and Excursions that make up most limousine rental firms' fleets? It could at least make a great tour bus for a rock band. Either way, it doesn't look as if you would need a fortune to get it back on the road.

This vehicle was probably built by Cotner-Bevington and used in the funeral trade. If you would like to bring it out of retirement, you need to call Vintage Automotive in Mountain Home, Idaho, which is where I found the car in 2004.

Below: Stageway Coaches built extra-long Chrysler limousines in the early 1970s, and this eight-door 1972 New Yorker is probably one of them. These cars were designed for airport work and had an emphasis on practicality rather than comfort. Some sort of industrial-strength air conditioning unit is on the roof of this limo, positioned in front of luggage storage boxes. The 1972 New Yorker had a large trunk, but not one large enough to accommodate this many passengers' luggage.

The picture was taken in the late 1990s on the outskirts of Kiowa, Kansas. The rural town is miles away from the nearest large airport, so presumably the car doesn't hail from these parts.

In 1956, anybody who was anybody wanted to be seen in a Cadillac Series 75 Fleetwood—America's only true production limousine at the time. The car sold remarkably well, with some 1,100 buyers finding the $6,300 needed to purchase one. This eight-passenger car came equipped with auxiliary seats and, in the case of the Imperial sedan, a hydraulic glass divide. Note the ridiculous homemade roof-rack bar—not a genuine GM option. However, the vehicle's air conditioning and power seats were.

This car was photographed in 2005 in Annandale, Minnesota.

Below: This six-passenger Cadillac Series 75 Fleetwood is a factory-built limo, one of 965 to find a customer in 1967. It initially cost well over $10,000, twice the price of the Fleetwood 65 sedan. Ignoring minimal surface rust and a couple of flat tires, this limo is in exceptionally good condition. It has retained all its glazing, one less headache for anyone intending to restore it.

This photograph was taken in 2001, when the car was a resident of a salvage yard in Casa Grande, Arizona.

Above: Henney-Packard hearses are rarer than hen's teeth, yet Junktown USA (a.k.a. French Lake Auto Parts) has a pair of them. Both appear to be 1950 models, and the one in the background is an unusual combination version. By the early 1950s, Henney was beginning to struggle. Although its Packard-based cars were well built, they didn't share the up-to-date styling of the Cadillacs. This hurt the company's market share. It built just a few hundred cars in 1950. Meanwhile, more than 2,000 Cadillac professional cars were built that year.

Left: Any funeral directors out there looking for something different to offer their customers? If so, look no further than this beautiful 1952 Superior Cadillac combination vehicle. It's basically a solid car and is crying out for a well-deserved restoration. What about those hard-to-find door-mounted coach lamps—aren't they enough to tempt you?

GM supplied 1,694 commercial chassis to the bodybuilding trade that year, with Superior taking the majority. A year later, the coachbuilder added a Pontiac to its lineup, a brand it had ignored since the 1940s.

This hearse was spotted at Johnson's AAA Wreckers in Chickasha, Oklahoma, where it was parked next to a similarly aged Cadillac hearse that had been converted into a pickup truck. Both may have been snapped up since this picture was taken.

Right: The lack of a side door and window indicate this Superior Cadillac was originally built for the U.S. military, which requested these specs at the time. The car's interior was also significantly simpler than those supplied to the civilian funeral trade. At some point, this Cadillac was used by the Arizona police, as suggested by the decal on its side. Presumably, it was the type of vehicle that takes human remains from a homicide scene to the police mortuary. The former hearse doesn't look too healthy itself, having been truly butchered during its stay in this Arizona yard.

Below: This car's overall condition can be summed up by the fact the cormorant on the front is wingless. Although the 1953 Henney-Packard is hidden from the main road, it appears to have attracted some unwanted visitors, who have smashed every single window and light. In 1936, Henney signed an exclusive agreement that ensured that it was the sole user of Packard's commercial chassis. The agreement lasted until the coachbuilder's demise in 1955.

This car was photographed in the late 1990s in Kansas. Judging by its poor state, I fear that the next funeral it attends will be its own.

The average hearse is in service for about twenty years and will likely carry about five thousand bodies. It's no wonder then that people shy away from these vehicles and the demand for used hearses is low. Perhaps that's why this wonderful 1953 Pontiac combination deteriorated to this condition and ended its days in an Illinois salvage yard.

Barnette, Miller-Meteor, Economy, and Superior were all building cars based on the Pontiac that year, and I'm not sure which is responsible for this model.

Unloved, uncared for, and unlikely to survive much longer, this is an unusual 1966 Cadillac hearse. It's actually a Classic limousine combination built by Miller-Meteor—one of the most respected names in the professional car industry. Combination vehicles like this were incredibly popular in the mid-1960s, as they were able to serve as both a hearse and ambulance. For funeral processions, drivers would snap on a pair of panels, complete with landau bows, to the rear side windows. They could be removed when required for ambulance duty, and a warning lamp was temporarily fitted to the roof. A black example is rare, though, as most were painted a lighter shade.

Miller-Meteor emerged in 1917 and built some of the industry's best hearses and ambulances until its demise in 1979. The name was resurrected in 1984, but with a different owner.

This car was found in an Illinois salvage yard where it sits in a pile of scrap metal—dangerously close to the crusher.

Left: This 1961 Buick Flxible Flxette limousine funeral coach was discovered in a tiny salvage yard in Winner, South Dakota. Other than a rusty tailgate, it is in superb condition and deserves to be put back on the road.

Flxible, perhaps better known for its buses, re-entered the funeral coach industry in 1959. The Flxette, introduced in 1960, was a big seller for the Ohio-based company. Like other professional vehicle offerings, it was built on a Buick chassis, but the shortest on the market. In other words, the Flxette was cheap, handled like a sedan, and offered respectable fuel economy. And a raised roof ensured that there was still adequate interior room. It was a winning formula, but Flxible only had the market to itself for one year. In 1961, Superior fought back with its compact Pontiac Consort.

Below: Despite being the last of the true coach-built cars—hand-crafted by skilled workers, rather than welded together by robots—secondhand professional vehicles don't carry a lot of value. When the vehicles reach the end of their working lives, they are generally worth no more than several hundred dollars. While some end up in the hands of collectors or find niche roles as band tour buses or tradesmen's vans, the majority reappear in the local salvage yard. This Superior-Pontiac Consort combination resides in an Illinois salvage yard, where it has been for more than two decades. Although it looks reasonably sound from the rear, the front no longer exists.

Superior's Pontiac hearses sold well because they were markedly cheaper than the Cadillac offerings.

Above: I found this well-camouflaged 1960 Superior-Pontiac ambulance on the outskirts of Tonopah, Nevada. There was nobody around to talk to, so I can't shed any light on the vehicle's history or future. As fond as I am of car-based ambulances, I understand why they were finally replaced by the spacious truck- and van-chassis offerings of today. This example may have an extended roof, but it couldn't have been the ideal environment in which to save someone's life.

Superior stopped producing the Pontiac ambulance in 1975.

Right: This 1958 Superior-Pontiac Criterion hightop ambulance, featuring a forty-six-inch roof, was originally owned by the U.S. Navy. Superior built five types of ambulances in 1958—three based on the Cadillac and two on the less expensive Pontiac Bonneville chassis.

The battered example you see here, found behind a gas station in the southeastern corner of Nevada, is in desperate need of some medical attention itself. Judging by the state of the front bumper, it has been involved in an accident and also needs an engine transplant. However, anyone brave enough to take on the restoration will be pleased that there are plenty of donor spare parts inside the car.

Below: The flower car is the rarest of all professional vehicles, as only a select number of funeral providers operated them. Even in a good year, the production of flower cars didn't reach double figures, making them reasonably collectible today.

You certainly won't find many in this poor state of repair, though. As far as I'm aware, Superior and Miller-Meteor's flower cars had four doors, leading me to believe this one was built by the McClain Sales and Leasing Company of Anderson, Indiana. It based its cars on the two-door Cadillac Coupe DeVille. This 1966 model, which still has its entire stainless-steel lining, was parked outside K&K Auto of Creston, Iowa, in 2005.

Below: The unique forward-sloping roof instantly identifies this 1966 Pontiac Bonneville as a Superior-built military-spec ambulance. These cars were manufactured on a tight budget, and their equipment levels were low. The ambulance is missing a central beacon and a single swiveling spotlight mounted over the driver compartment. By the mid-1960s, a growing number of ambulances were built with fiberglass roofs instead of steel. The material was light, lowering the car's center of gravity and improving its drivability. However, this model, like all military cars, had a conventional steel roof. It is one of several professional cars in an Elmwood, Nebraska, salvage yard.

Above: Whoever painted the transfers and wording on this 1966 Oldsmobile 98–based professional car was seriously deluded if he thought his handiwork made it look like the *Ghost Busters* ambulance. The effort is a bit like welding shut the doors of an orange 1980 Honda Civic, painting the confederate flag on the roof, and climbing in through the windows.

Although unable to find the coachbuilder's name on the car, I think it's a Cotner-Bevington. To my knowledge, this was the only company using Oldsmobile donor vehicles at the time. This car is another combination coach and has somehow managed to keep hold of its snap-on window panels. (Incidentally, the real star of the *Ghost Busters* film was a far more desirable 1959 Miller-Meteor Cadillac Futura.)

Left: Car-based ambulances were selling steadily in the 1960s, but a decade later van- and truck-type ambulances were all the rage. Then in the mid-1970s, when the auto industry downsized its cars, new federal ambulance design regulations were passed. These regulations spelled the end for car-based ambulances and combination vehicles. The result was devastating for the coach-building industry, and several manufacturers were forced to close their doors.

This 1960s-era Cadillac Classic ambulance is one of several professional cars I found in Ace Auto Salvage in Tonica, Illinois, in 2005. The fact that it can cope with the weight of a car on its roof is testament to Miller-Meteor's build quality.

Right: Let's hope the wooden church here doesn't burn down because I don't think the Manhattan volunteer firefighters are going to be much help—at least not in this car-based fire truck. This amazing Nevada ghost town is definitely worth a visit. In 1906, when gold, silver, and copper were being pulled out of the ground, four thousand people lived in Manhattan. The town had numerous banks, schools, saloons, and certainly a number of brothels. By the 1940s, most of the residents had left, although some seem to have forgotten their cars. If you look carefully, you'll find a number of similarly aged automotive remains scattered around the place.

Below: Old abandoned cars are frequently used as promotional devices by antique stores, restaurants, and other businesses—often with an advertising placard on their roof or a hand-painted sign on the door. However, people don't normally go to this much effort. Somebody clearly invested a lot of time turning a 1947 Chevy Stylemaster four-door sedan into the "Kerr County party patrol" car. It has been parked outside Neighbors Gin Mill and Dance Hall in Ingram, Texas, and is presumably the place to call "in case of a dead party."

You didn't want to see this Ford state trooper in your mirror while driving through the Tennessee countryside in the late 1960s. Once upon a time, this 1967 model had under the hood a highly tuned and very desirable V-8, which has long since found a new home. Having been put out to pasture in the early 1970s, the car's criminal-catching days are truly over. Yet this car would definitely make an interesting restoration project for someone.

Blinded in one eye, this 1936 Ford pickup truck gradually disappears into the undergrowth of a south Texas salvage yard. A suspicious rattling noise coming from the grass prevented me from getting any closer, so I didn't investigate whether there is still a V-8 lurking under that hood. The 1936 Ford pickup didn't look a whole lot different from the previous year's model, with a slightly modified radiator grille as the only notable visual difference. By that stage, Ford had produced three million trucks.

Note the obligatory school bus in the background—no junkyard is complete without at least one.

Left: Unlike many of Nevada's mining camps, Belmont had an abundance of wood, water, rock, and clay, allowing townsfolk to construct substantial, fireproof buildings. That's a good thing, considering the state of this fire engine. However, by the time this truck arrived in Belmont, the town was virtually nonexistent. Belmont effectively died one hundred years ago, and since then only a handful of people have lived there.

According to the California chapter of the Society for the Preservation and Appreciation of Antique Motor Fire Apparatus in America (SPAAMFAA), the high-low pattern on the hood louvers indicates that this vehicle is most likely a 1930s Seagrave. However, the society notes the bullet-type headlights are probably not original because the Ohio-based manufacturer preferred flat-fronted, large-diameter lights.

Below: How's this for an impressive lineup of ancient workhorses? It includes an International, a Diamond T, a Chevrolet, and an REO. The International, a C-Series, probably dates to 1936. That year International Harvester Corporation (IHC) churned out over 86,000 trucks, enough to give the company an 11 percent share of the market and rank it the third-largest truck manufacturer in the United States.

This private collection of commercial vehicles sits by a busy roadside in Davenport, Iowa. All are pretty rusty and appear to have retired a decade or two ago, but are nonetheless structurally sound.

Above: How's this for a severe case of automotive acne? It's common for desert finds to have an occasional bullet hole in them, but this one looks like it's been shot with a machine gun. I would love to tell you what it is, but this one has me beat. Just as intriguing is how exactly it, and the car in the background, got out here in the Nevada desert, just a stone's throw from U.S. Highway 95. Did they simply break down and get left here by their disgruntled owners, or were they dragged here by someone? I guess we'll never know.

The historic derelict buildings in Belmont, Nevada, not only have to survive the occasional fire and the passing of time, but they also have local vandals to contend with. According to one of the few residents still living in this town, hooligans have been known to chain buildings to pickup trucks and then drive off—razing the building to the ground in the process. I wonder if that's what happened to the tumbled barn in the background. This prewar Chevrolet truck has stood the test of time better than many of the town's wooden structures. Since there aren't any sidelights fitted to the fenders, I'm guessing it's a 1939 model.

Trucks have a much longer life expectancy than cars in rural America, so it's not uncommon to see 1950s-era pickups, flatbeds, and tippers still trundling down unpaved byways in the boondocks. I wouldn't be surprised at all to learn this 1937 Ford workhorse was still earning a living on a nearby farm into the twenty-first century. After all, it is still relatively intact, and the majority of its tires remain fully inflated. But its real working days are over, and its reward for sixty years of hard labor is banishment to a salvage yard in Wymore, Nebraska. If it were a real workhorse, it would have been turned into glue by now.

With the lettering "Rhyolite" on the tank, this 1940s Ford truck was once based at the famous ghost town of the same name. Gold was discovered in Rhyolite, Nevada, at the start of the twentieth century, and before long, thousands of money-hungry hopefuls set up camp here. At its peak, the town had ten thousand residents, serviced by countless brothels and casinos, three public swimming pools, and two schools.

However, the gold the town was built on soon ran out, as did the residents. The last one died in 1924, leaving behind nothing but crumbling buildings. Today, there are just two complete structures standing in Rhyolite: the train station and a house built from fifty-one thousand whisky bottles. Even this truck has now left Rhyolite, moving to another Nevada mining town: Goldfield.

Rhyolite, Nevada, was such a successful city in its heyday that promoters easily attracted no less than three railroads. Then the Las Vegas and Tonopah Railroad invested a cool million dollars in the brick building you see in the background, dubbed "The Dearborn Street Station of the West." However, the line was abandoned in the early 1920s, and the station briefly became a casino before being abandoned.

This late 1940s Ford truck also appears to be ownerless, unless you count the litter of kittens that were calling it home when this photograph was taken.

When Route 66 ceased to be a national highway, it was the end of the road for many of the communities that lined its path. Some of the hardest hit were in the Texas panhandle and parts of western Oklahoma, where the road was replaced by Interstate 40. Local businesses, which existed on passing trade, were the first to feel the pinch when traffic flow became no more than a trickle. Motels were forced to turn off their neon lights, gas stations stopped pumping, and diners went out of business. Texola, on the Texas-Oklahoma border, was one of the towns affected and is where I discovered this 1940s half-ton Ford Series 7GC sedan delivery. The town is a shadow of its former self, with numerous derelict buildings.

A couple of miles down the road from here, a whole section of the original Route 66 now has trees and shrubs growing through the asphalt.

Aside from the sagging wooden framework around its cargo area, this circa 1948 Chevy two-ton COE is actually doing remarkably well for its age. This truck was Chevrolet's first postwar creation, but not its first COE design. That was launched almost a decade earlier. Despite the 1948 model's new look, there was no change to the engines. Buyers got the choice between a 216-cubic-inch six-cylinder producing 90 brake horsepower or a 235-cubic-inch engine pumping out 105 brake horsepower. This truck was found just off Nevada's Highway 50, nicknamed "America's Loneliest Road."

I stumbled upon this rare 1949 Pontiac Streamliner sedan delivery while trying to locate Flathead Salvage in Somers, Montana. The vehicle was parked by the side of the road and had a very reasonable price of $3,500 posted in the window. This was Pontiac's first commercial vehicle since 1928, and only 2,488 were built. It was based on the station wagon, but had a two-door design with a curbside opening rear door for access to the cargo area. Buyers had a choice between six- or eight-cylinder engines.

Flathead Salvage was closed when I finally found it, but the journey there wasn't wasted.

This colorful duo was photographed in northern Montana in 2005. The World War II military Dodge WC (on the right), complete with snowplow attachment, appears to have recently stopped working for a living. And being this close to the Rockies, you can bet it has had an exhausting life. Between 1940 and 1945, Dodge built more than 250,000 military trucks, with a vast array of bodies. The WC featured a civilian cab, but used unique front-end sheet metal. All but a handful of them had four-wheel drive.

The Ford pickup truck next to it also hails from the 1940s.

My guess is that this truck was the victim of an over-enthusiastic amateur, who probably started the work years ago when late 1940s Chevy trucks were pretty worthless. It probably was a good practice vehicle because pickups are relatively easy to chop. Also, if the experiment went wrong, the fabricator wouldn't have kissed a fortune goodbye. For some reason, the task was abandoned in its infancy and hardly any of the joints are welded. Perhaps the customizer realized he'd bitten off more than he could chew, or just lost interest and moved onto another project. Either way, it's a shame because the truck probably had plenty of potential.

At some point, it was hauled to a junkyard in Marfa, Texas, where it awaits its fate.

Above: If not for being pinned to the ground by a tree, this early 1950s Studebaker 2R truck cab probably would have been crushed by now. The 2R series debuted in 1949 and was an immediate success. With its four-year production run, it became the top-producing Studebaker truck. Although 2R production ceased in 1953, its cab (the C cab) continued to be manufactured for another six years on light-duty trucks and another eleven years on heavy-duty trucks. The last Studebaker commercial vehicles rolled off the line in 1964.

Above: I found this discarded cab dumped in a ravine, in the shadow of a lonesome Joshua tree. It appears to be an International, either a prewar K series or a postwar KB. It's located on the outskirts of Goldfield, Nevada, although a century ago this spot would have been right in the middle of town. Over the years, a succession of serious floods and fires destroyed much of this area, and it was never rebuilt. You can make out a couple of surviving wooden buildings in the background.

Goldfield is the only town I've ever found where abandoned cars appear to outnumber people. So it should come as no surprise to learn that this is where I spent all of six thousand dollars on a second home. Ironically, I must be one of the few property owners in Goldfield who doesn't have any rusting vehicles on blocks in their front yard.

Right: The temperature in Moab, Utah, reaches triple figures in mid-July, and I would have happily fed a whole pile of quarters into this ancient soda machine if it worked. But like the IHC truck in the background, it hasn't been powered up in decades and now awaits its fate in Bert's Auto Supply.

The truck is a Model L, 1950 to 1952 vintage, and features a distinctive grille and one-piece windscreen. Originally, it was equipped with an overhead valve inline, six-cylinder engine, which was good for 101 horsepower, compared with its predecessor's 82 horsepower output.

Right: Shortly after September 11, 2001, the United States became a nation united by the Stars and Stripes. For the next few months, nearly every car and truck on the road proudly displayed the flag. In fact, even the occasional nonroad-worthy vehicle doubled as a flagpole. This patriotic Ford, photographed somewhere in Mississippi, is a 1955 F-100. It is sitting next to a 1954 version, which is also for sale.

The original 1953 F-100 was the product of thirty million dollars of research and development—an investment that certainly paid off. In its first year, 116,437 were built, and by 1955 the figure had risen to 124,842.

Below: The dentistry on this Idaho-based 1952 Ford half-ton F-1 panel van is almost perfect, but unfortunately, the rest of the truck hasn't fared so well. It seems to be missing an engine, a transmission, a hood, an interior, two axles, and plenty more. This was the fifth and final year for the F-1 (the original F series), but it certainly wasn't the end of its story. Thirty years later, the F series was the best-selling vehicle in America. In 1995, it overtook the Volkswagen Bug as the world's best-selling vehicle ever. During Ford Motor Company's first one one-hundred-years, one out of every ten vehicles produced by the company was an F-series truck.

This homemade 1953 pickup truck started out as one of the 2,000 Cadillac hearses built that year. But when it retired from the funeral business, its next owner probably decided it would be more useful with a flatbed than a roof, so out came the angle grinder. A surprising number of professional cars of this era ended up as trucks, and I've unearthed a handful of them on my travels. This Las Vegas example isn't the best conversion I've ever seen (notice the shoddy plywood bulkhead). What's the deal with all those bottles, I wonder?

I can't think of a better place to camp than Vintage Automotive of Mountain Home, Idaho. If yard owner Jim Hines rented this camper out, I'd be the first to book it for a week. After all, check out the scenery right on your doorstep! The camper looks like it started out as a 1957 Studebaker Commander pickup, but that's impossible because that vehicle never existed. So presumably this homemade conversion is based on a passenger car, maybe a station wagon. Although it appears to be a reasonably professional conversion, I'm not so sure about those rear-view mirrors—and what's mounted on the cab's roof?

This would make quite an interesting restoration project and would certainly turn some heads at a campground.

Here's a commercial vehicle that you don't see too many of—a 1958 Chevy sedan delivery. This panel van shared the same general styling as the Delray passenger car and came with the six-cylinder engine as standard. However, those drivers who were in a rush to make their deliveries could opt for either the 283- or 358-cubic-inch V-8 instead.

This photograph was taken in 2001 at Vintage Auto Salvage of Bradford, Arkansas. Although yard owner Ed Summar clearly puts a lot of time into keeping the yard's grass impeccable, I don't think he's noticed the plants growing inside the van and engine bay.

Surely one of the most stylish commercial vehicles ever built was the 1959 Chevrolet El Camino. GM's half-car, half-truck was an attempt to cash in on the success of Ford's Ranchero, which was launched two years earlier. The El Camino was based on the Impala and shared its distinctive wings and cat's-eye taillights. However, the vehicle was only around for a couple of years, disappearing until 1964 when it returned with Chevelle underpinnings.

El Camino translates as "the road" in Spanish, but I'd be surprised if this one ever sees another road beneath its wheels. It was photographed just off Highway 93 in the northwest corner of Arizona.

Esmeralda County, Nevada, has literally thousands of gold mines, but only hundreds of residents. In fact, it's the least populated county in the state. Yet considering how so few people live here, the county has an abnormally large number of abandoned vehicles. I traveled the county's dirt roads with local historian Big Bob Plock, who guided me around the abandoned mineshafts to a number of abandoned vehicles—including this early 1960s Ford Econoline panel van.

While taking the photograph, I disturbed a rattlesnake basking in the Nevada sun, but luckily it was more scared of me than vice versa.

Finally, no book on abandoned autos could be complete without a dedication to the canine car protector: the dreaded junkyard dog. Fearless and mean, these aggressive, snarling, bloodthirsty beasts strike terror into the hearts of any junkyard junkie. Well actually, that's a bit of a myth. Yes, I've had one or two close calls over the years, but I have to admit that the average guard dog is a big softy. From my experience, the majority are more interested in licking than biting. Then again, I'm wandering around the yard with permission. They likely have a different attitude toward someone on an off-hours illegal parts-finding mission.

Although the most common breeds of junkyard dog seem to be the German shepherd and rottweiler, the majority are mixed-breed mutts. Not every yard opts for a canine guard, though. I know of one North Dakota business with a flock of junkyard sheep and I've had half my camera bag eaten by a junkyard goat. Then I was spat on by a junkyard lama and pecked at by a gaggle of hissing guard geese. But my favorite of all has to be the central California yard with a junkyard cat—and the highest, most secure perimeter fence I've ever seen.

INDEX